Tabari

MAKERS OF ISLAMIC CIVILIZATION

Series editor: Farhan A. Nizami

This series, conceived by the Oxford Centre for Islamic Studies, is jointly published by Oxford University Press and I.B. Tauris. The books in the series, written by leading scholars in the field, aim to provide an introduction to outstanding figures in the history of Islamic civilization. They will serve as the essential first point of reference for study of the persons, events and ideas that have shaped the Islamic world and the cultural resources on which Muslims continue to draw.

Tabari

Ulrika Mårtensson

Oxford Centre for Islamic Studies

OXFORD
UNIVERSITY PRESS

OXFORD
UNIVERSITY PRESS

YMCA Library Building, Jai Singh Road, New Delhi 110 001

Oxford University Press is a department of the University of Oxford.
It furthers the University's objective of excellence in research, scholarship,
and education by publishing worldwide in

Oxford New York
Auckland Cape Town Dar es Salaam Hong Kong Karachi Kuala Lumpur Madrid
Melbourne Mexico City Nairobi New Delhi Shanghai Taipei Toronto

With offices in
Argentina Austria Brazil Chile Czech Republic France Greece Guatemala Hungary
Italy Japan Poland Portugal Singapore South Korea Switzerland Thailand Turkey
Ukraine Vietnam

Published in India by Oxford University Press

First published 2009

ISBN-13: 978-0-19-806301-8
ISBN-10: 0-19-806301-6

For sale only in India, Pakistan, Bangladesh, Sri Lanka, Nepal, Bhutan, and Myanmar

Cover: tile image adapted from photo by Yahya Michot

Typeset in Garamond 11.5/13.8
Printed in India by Parangat Offset, New Delhi 110 020
Published by Oxford University Press
YMCA Library Building, Jai Singh Road, New Delhi 110 001

Contents

	List of maps	vi
	Preface	1
1	Tabari's life and works	7
2	Reading the *History*	40
3	Tabari's *History*	55
4	Conclusion	145
5	Further reading	151
	Index	170

List of maps*

1 *Core territories of the 'Abbasid empire, mostly inherited from the Sassanids; cities where Tabari lived and studied* 10

2 *Rebellions and rival dynasties which weakened the power of the 'Abbasid state* 14

3 *The Sawad* 42

4 *Arabia on the eve of Islam; the Byzantine and Sassanid empires; territories of the Ghassan and Lakhm tribes* 99

5 *Expansion of territories under Muslim rule during the Companions' caliphates; sites of important battles* 101

6 *The Umayyad and 'Abbasid caliphates at the peak of their power* 123

* Cartography by Alexander Kent, PhD., FBCart.S., FRGS.

Preface

By any standard, Abu Ja'far Muhammad b. Jarir b. Yazid al-Tabari (839–923), was an extraordinarily erudite and prolific scholar in several classical Islamic disciplines – Prophetic tradition (*ḥadīth*); interpretation of the Qur'an; Islamic jurisprudence; and history. Only a few of some 27 titles attributed to him have come down to us. These are: *Tahdhib al-athar*, a critical assessment of Prophetic and Companion traditions; *Ikhtilaf al-fuqaha'*, a survey of the main points of controversy among jurists; *Jami' al-bayan*, a commentary on the Qur'an; *Ṣarīḥ al-sunna*, a brief 'profession of faith'; and *Ta'rikh al-rusul wa-l-muluk*, a history of prophethood and statehood from Creation to the 'Abbasid caliphate in the year 915. All five have been published in scholarly modern editions, and some partially translated into English or other Western languages. Only *Ta'rikh al-rusul wa-l-muluk* (hereafter '*History*') has been translated into English in its entirety. It is a testimony to its brilliance as a product of medieval Islamic civilization, and its importance as a major source of historical information about early Islamic history and the Sassanid (Persian) empire, that its translation was sponsored by UNESCO, with support from the American National Endowment for the Humanities. The project took almost thirty years and resulted in forty volumes, published between 1985 and 2007. Details of the scholarly editions of Tabari's works and the translations of them are given in 'Further reading' (below, pp. 151–160).

To try to do justice to the quality and range of Tabari's works in a short book about him is a hugely daunting task: one has to select. I have focused on the *History*. In doing so I have also tried to show where it stands in relation to the other major works, and pointed out the common concerns and methodology which give to the surviving Tabari corpus a quite remarkable philosophical coherence and solidity.

Tabari's overall preoccupation in the *History* is rational *vs.* irrational imperial government, the factors that promote imperial strength and those that promote decline. The functional value of his historical analysis may be guessed by the fact that Ottoman sultans acquired complete copies of the work: this is why the best manuscripts are held in libraries in Istanbul. An instructive comparison is Edward Gibbon's (1737–1794) *History of the Decline and Fall of the Roman Empire* (originally published in six volumes, 1776–88). It is about half the length of Tabari's *History*, covering the 1350 years from the rise of the Roman empire in the second century to the fall of Constantinople in 1453. Both Tabari and Gibbon were rationalists, but where Tabari saw his religion as the source of rationality and imperial strength, Gibbon perceived Christianity as the source of unreason and, consequently, imperial weakness. Both relied on primary sources. This makes them early representatives of the modern science of history, which is distinguished from its antecedents precisely by the use of primary sources. Tabari's extensive (and subtle) use of primary sources or 'reports' (*akhbār*, sing. *khabar*), is the reason why the *History* remains one of the richest sources of information about the Sassanid dynasty; the Arab kingdoms of Syria, Mesopotamia and Yemen before Islam; the Companion caliphs; the disputes over succession which divided the Muslim community politically and religiously; the ʻAbbasid seizure of power first from the Umayyads and then from the ʻAlids; and ʻAbbasid glory and decline. On the Sassanid period and the Companion caliphs especially, Tabari is unrivalled in numbers of sources and detail, which is why later Islamic historians depended on the *History* as the definitive text on the emergence and formative history of Islam.

In contemporary studies of Tabari's works, methodology is a recurrent theme. On the *History* the present scholarly consensus appears to be that Tabari did not seek to explain historical processes in terms of economic and social structures and mechanisms, but rather to evaluate the moral qualities of individual historical actors. To the extent the scope of this book allows, I question that consensus.

In his Qur'an commentary, Tabari holds that any explanation always expresses the subjective concerns of the one explaining, at the same time as it expresses something about the matter explained. Tabari applied this notion to textual interpretation of the Qur'an; I will argue that it is applicable to his other works including the *History*, insofar as it presents reports with a clear explanatory objective. I hope to show that Tabari's methodologies (and related explanations) in the major disciplines – Prophetic tradition, jurisprudence, Qur'an interpretation, and history – express his personal concerns, which are in turn linked to his preferred 'rational' policy for the state and state administration. Since it is through historical examples that Tabari distinguishes rational and irrational administrative practices, this approach gives the *History* a central role in understanding Tabari's whole oeuvre. Tabari was personally concerned to explain the causes of the problems that he witnessed in the ʻAbbasid system, namely that the state was rapidly losing control over the provinces as well as its central territories and its armed forces.

Most of the contents of the *History* that I refer to in this book illustrate Tabari's analysis of the socio-political and economic problems of his time. Examples are given from narratives about rulers, pre-Islamic and Islamic, about material issues such as land and taxation, and legal–political issues such as covenant, social contract, and succession. I will argue that for Tabari, 'good governance' equals 'rational governance', which required that rulers and administrators balance material resources so as to meet the needs and interests of the ruling institutions and their related social groups. I will show, with reference to Tabari's other works, that his methodology is related to his ideas about 'good governance' in two ways, both linked to his concept of rationality.

Firstly, on the role of reason as source of knowledge, Tabari held a middle position between the strict 'rationalists' (who rejected tradition as source of law, scriptural interpretation and theology) and the strict 'traditionalists' (who sought to base law, interpretation and theology as much as possible on the texts of scripture and tradition). Tabari's position was that the texts provide basic legal principles together with some concrete examples of their application, and therefore reason should be continuously exercised on those texts in order to derive laws and ethical guidance; and to solve issues without textual foundation, reason could be applied to deduce solutions by reference to analogous cases.

Secondly, since Tabari wanted his work to inspire rational practices, objectivity (what we might call 'positivism') was the means and ends of his scholarly method: sources should be identifiable, facts verifiable and methods repeatable. His analysis was irreverent; he spared no one from critical examination. However, since his critique was based on objective principles, sources and methods, it could not be dismissed as subjective opinion. I hope this study will give the reader a sense of Tabari's modern outlook; to me, he comes across as a medieval proponent of today's global standards of 'good governance' and, indeed, good science.

The policy-oriented concern in Tabari's works is matched by the profound psychological insight and compassion that characterize his narratives. This could reflect his less well known intellectual pursuits – we know from bibliographical notices that he wrote treatises on ethics and dream interpretation. It may be this side of his scholarly formation that makes his works so enduring – without the compassion and wit, his penetrating view of human affairs might have been unbearable. He is unsparing in exposing human mistakes but merciful in conveying how difficult it is for human beings to estimate the possible outcomes of their choices and actions – only God has such knowledge. Tabari's narrative technique in the *History* makes the reader experience just how partial and limited our understanding of a situation really is: he first presents a report that gives the reader a sense of certitude about why something happened, and then another report which subverts the first, seeing the same event from another viewpoint and with a different emotional response. This technique, it seems, corresponded to Tabari's position on the issue of human free will versus divine predestination: being human is choosing among an unknown but finite number of possible courses of action, whose outcomes appear reasonable and predictable only with hindsight. Such 'after-thinking' is the service which history can render and which, if heeded, can sometimes guide the human exercise of power away from error. It is a reflection of Tabari's compassionate side that, after narrating the reign and death of a caliph, he always ends by listing the good things the individual is remembered for, reminding us how hard it is, from within the flow of events, to make the right choices, and that there are good things to be said about every human life.

The book is divided into four parts. Part 1 presents basic information about Tabari's life and works and related research problems, and his methodology. In Part 2, I discuss the methodological, conceptual and historical presuppositions that are necessary to analyse Tabari's works, especially the *History*, effectively. Part 3 discusses the *History*, illustrating the relationship between material resources and legal principles, and Tabari's historical analysis. The concluding Part 4, as well as observations on the continued use and significance of Tabari's works, gives an overview of Tabari's historical methodology and analysis in relation to his other major works so as to illustrate the significance of the *History* for understanding Tabari's scholarly corpus as a whole.

In conformity with the series format, I have minimized references and notes. Similarly, I have used transliteration only when citing published works, when presenting a name or title formally 'in Arabic', and when using an Arabic term with a restricted, technical sense. Inevitably, in a work by diverse hands on the scale of *History*, there are variations in the translation of certain terms: in some instances I have preferred (and explained) my own translation. In these instances and where I have amended or omitted from the cited text, the alteration is shown like this: {omitted or altered text}.

Finally, I would like to express thanks to the series editor, Farhan Nizami, for commissioning the work, and his two anonymous readers for their very helpful criticisms of an early draft. I am grateful to the Norwegian University of Science and Technology's Department of Archaeology and Religious Studies for generous research leave. I also thank Stefano Bisighin for his valuable comments. Lastly, my editor, Jamil Qureshi, and my partner, Lionel Sacks, have engaged in this book in ways that have improved it significantly: I am deeply indebted to them. All shortcomings are entirely my own.

June, 2009

Ulrika Mårtensson
Trondheim

Part 1

Tabari's life and works

LIFE

Tabari's name (in full, Abū Jaʿfar Muḥammad ibn Jarīr ibn Yazīd al-Ṭabarī) is a natural starting point for a short biography. 'Abu Ja'far' (lit., 'Ja'far's father') follows the common patronymic pattern, naming parents after their first male child. However, there is no information about Tabari having had children. He never married and is reported to have said that he never 'let down his pants for either a forbidden or a permitted (sexual activity)' (*History*, i/Rosenthal. 34).[1] This was supposedly said when he was a young man, and it is not known if he ever changed his habits on this matter. In any case, a patronymic need not refer to a biological child; it is sometimes given to young boys (or girls), an affectionate nickname that simply sticks. The main reason that Tabari did not marry was his devotion to scholarship. Certainly, he was a handsome man:

---

[1] References to the *History*: lower-case roman numerals signify volume number, followed by the translator's name, then page number(s).

His physical appearance showed a darkish brown complexion and large eyes, as well as a long beard [...]. [H]is hair and beard stayed quite black until he was in his eighties. He was tall and lean. His leanness may have contributed to his vigour and good health throughout his long life. (*History*, i/Rosenthal. 39–40)

Regarding attitudes to women, Tabari held what would nowadays be called a gender theory of 'sameness'. He is quoted as declaring that women and men are intellectual equals, and that women could therefore serve as judges in Shari'a law.[1] Judging from some reports he includes in the *History*, he seems to have had a keen appreciation of the forces of sexual attraction. A fine example is the conversation he reports (see *History*, xvi/Hillenbrand, 21–2) between the 'Alid heir Zayd b. 'Ali (d. 740) and Umm 'Amr, an older woman with whom Zayd was initially infatuated. Though always chaste and courteous, the exchange between them is refreshingly frank and direct. Umm 'Amr declines Zayd's proposal of marriage, guiding his appreciation of her physical and social charms to those of her daughter, whom Zayd marries and with whom also 'he was madly in love'.

If the patronymic 'Abu Ja'far' is slightly mysterious, 'al-Tabari' is wholly uncomplicated: it refers to his place of birth, the town Amul in the province Tabaristan, on the southern shore of the Caspian Sea, where his family owned lands. From 529, this region had been a province (then called Mazandaran) in the Persian-ruled Sassanid empire (226–651), with its own, local branches of the Sassanid royal family as rulers, alongside other non-Sassanid noble families. Following the Muslim conquest (640), the local Sassanid and other nobility remained in place, indeed until as late as 1349.

---

1 See Cook, *The Koran*, 104, where he refers to the famous jurist and Sufi, Ibn al-'Arabi, who quotes Tabari on this issue. Ibn al-'Arabi took the opposite and more common view that (on grounds of intellectual inferiority) women cannot serve as judges.

However, further conquests in the region (from 644) meant that the local nobility had to make room also for the Arab conquerors. After the ʿAbbasid rise to power (in about 750), Tabaristan was nominally a province of the ʿAbbasid caliphate, but was in fact ruled by virtually autonomous governors. Alongside the Sassanid and other noble families, ʿAlids of the Zaydi school came to occupy a special position in Tabaristan. Between 864 and 928, a Zaydi branch of the Hasanid ʿAlids ruled in parts of the region, and Husaynid ʿAlids from 916/17 to 948/49.

The name by which Tabari was most often referred to was 'Ibn Jarir', 'son of Jarir'. Jarir is an Arabic name, and all Tabari's paternal relatives had Arab Muslim names, distinct from the Persian families of Tabaristan. Rosenthal therefore suggests that his father's family descended from the first Arab colonists; Bosworth, however, inclines towards Persian descent.[1] The biographical sources contain no definitive information about his mother and her family, who may well have been Persians. Both the *History* and the Qur'an commentary show that Tabari was familiar with the Persian language; but this he could have learned through studies. A curious reference, dating to more than sixty years after Tabari's death, claims that his maternal relatives were Shiʿis, i.e. of the ʿAlid families. This was dismissed as slander by the medieval biographer Yaqut (d. 1229), an assessment with which Rosenthal agrees (*History*, i/Rosenthal. 13). In sum, regarding Tabari's ancestry there remain uncertainties.

Already as a child Tabari displayed an unusual gift for scholarly learning. According to Yaqut, Tabari in his old age claimed to have memorized the Qur'an by the age of seven,

---

[1] *History* i/Rosenthal. 12; Bosworth, 'The Persian contribution', 225.

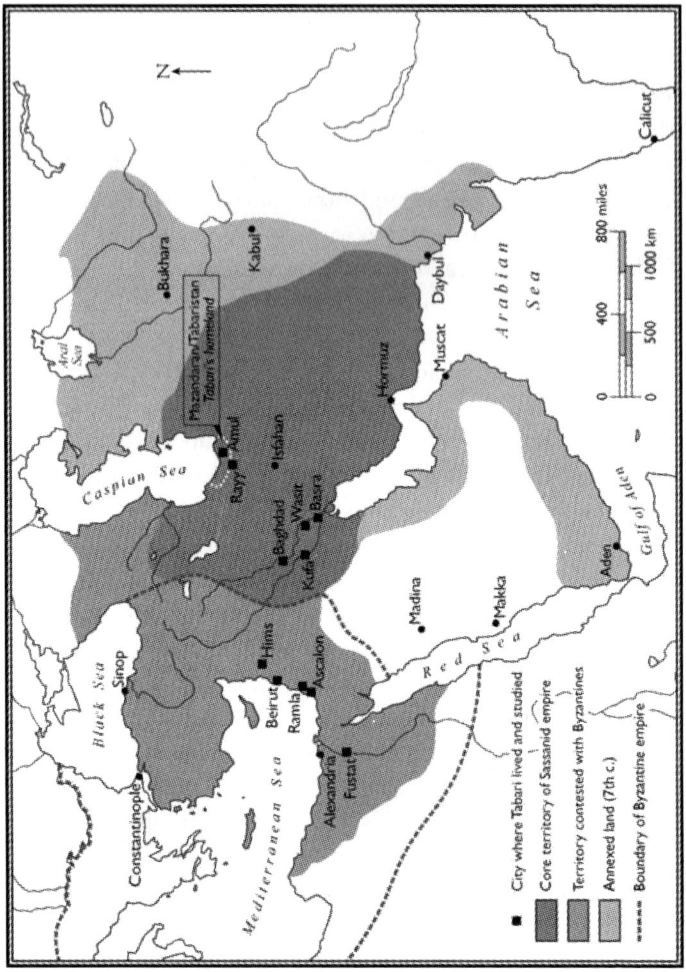

Map 1. *Core territories of the 'Abbasid empire, mostly inherited from the Sassanids; cities where Tabari lived and studied*

first led the prayer by the age of eight, and first written down Prophetic traditions by the age of nine. When he was twelve years old he left Amul for the centres of learning. He spent five years at Rayy, the metropolis of northern Persia at the time, studying, among other subjects, the biography of the Prophet. At seventeen, he moved on from Rayy to the splendid 'Abbasid capital Baghdad, where he spent one year. Then he moved to the other Iraqi centres of learning, the old garrison cities of Kufa, Basra, and Wasit. After about two years, he returned to Baghdad and stayed for eight years. Then he departed again, for Beirut, Hims, Ramla, Ascalon, and finally Egypt, where he arrived in 867. In 870, he returned again to Baghdad, where he spent the remaining fifty-odd years of his life writing scholarly works. He enjoyed financial independence, enabling him to pursue his studies as he wished. This was made possible by his inheritance of his father's share in the family lands. He would receive farm produce by caravan from Amul, via Khurasan, to Baghdad, where he traded the goods. His physical contacts with Amul were, however, scarce; during this half century in Baghdad, he visited Tabaristan only twice, the last time in 902/903.

During his second stay in Baghdad (some time between 858/9 and 862, when he was in his twenties), Tabari acquired a position in the uppermost ranks of the state administration. On recommendation, the vizier 'Ubayd Allah b. Yahya b. al-Khaqan (d. 877) appointed him to tutor his son. The Khaqans were a family of secretaries of state, of Persian origin related to '*abna' Khurasan*', 'the sons of Khurasan', professional soldiers from the province Khurasan who had contributed to bringing the 'Abbasid dynasty to power in 749 and 750, and thereafter served as one of several military groups at the caliph's service. The Khaqans continued to hold Tabari in high esteem. From 870 onwards, they were allied with another secretarial family, Banu al-Jarrah, who had become powerful enough to control appointments of scribes and viziers. Towards the end of Tabari's life, Banu al-Jarrah had another son of 'Ubayd Allah, Muhammad al-Khaqani, appointed as vizier, who offered Tabari positions first as judge, and then within the *maẓālim* courts (roughly, 'court of grievances'). He graciously declined both offers, as he wished to continue his studies and writing. Al-Khaqani's rule was disastrous and lasted only one year (912–13), after which Banu al-Jarrah appointed the famous vizier 'Ali b. 'Isa, one of their own kin. 'Ali b. 'Isa held office during two periods, 913–17 and 927–28. It seems that Tabari was on as good terms with him as with the Khaqans; for example, the vizier had Tabari looked after when he was ill, and supported him against his major opponents, the Hanbalis.

Even though the biographers cast Tabari in overwhelmingly favourable terms, he did have opponents in Baghdad, especially among activists of the emerging Hanbali school, who were vying for recognition from scholars and statesmen. There are different opinions (see below, pp. 152–153) on how serious Hanbali enmity to Tabari really was, whether it was a real threat or just a nuisance. What is clear is that the Hanbalis attacked Tabari for his views on theology (*kalām*), and accused him of sympathies with the 'Alid Shi'a. Tabari, according to Dominique Sourdel, wrote his creed, *Ṣarīḥ al-sunna* ('The Purity of the *Sunna*'), to demonstrate that the Hanbalis' charges were baseless.[1]

Generally regarding the Shi'a, there were controversies of simultaneously doctrinal and political nature, concerning whether Shi'ism should be recognized as a school of theology and jurisprudence, and what status the 'Alids, descendants of the Prophet's cousin 'Ali ibn Abi Talib and daughter Fatima, could claim. In Tabari's days, there were three broad Shi'i positions *vis-à-vis* the 'Abbasid caliphate.

---

1 Sourdel, *Profession de foi*, 177. See also: Gilliot, *Exégèse Coranique*, 60; Melchert, *Formation*, 194.

Firstly, the position, identified with *Imam* Ja'far al-Sadiq (702–765) and the later Imami or Ja'fari school, according to which 'Ali and his sons are the true *Imam*s, who should have been recognized as such by all Muslims. However, after the 'Abbasid rise to power, the Imamis interpreted the Imamate as spiritual leadership, allowing them to recognize the 'Abbasid caliphs as worldly rulers and postpone the advent of the true Imamate and just government to the end of time. This was coupled to the doctrine that the *Imam*s were free of sin. Secondly, there were the Zaydis, named after Zayd b. 'Ali (695–740), who did not hold the *Imam*s to be free of sin, and did not blame other Muslims for not having sided with 'Ali and the *Imam*s. Instead, they believed that the *Imam* had to prove himself worthy of allegiance, by establishing just government, if necessary by rebellion. This approach allowed the Zaydis to establish regional governments, in Tabaristan and Yemen, while leaving the 'Abbasids to rule the centre. The third position was the Isma'ili, which militantly resisted any government not led by an 'Alid descending from Ja'far's son, the seventh *Imam*, Isma'il. Isma'ilism took shape as an underground propaganda campaign (*da'wa*) for a just caliphate under the *Imam*. The movement originated in the Iraqi city of Kufa, from where it spread to Yemen, and to North Africa in 762. Here the Arab leadership linked up with Berber tribes and established a military power base, which eventually allowed them to establish the Fatimid caliphate (909–1171), rivalling that of the 'Abbasids. Tabari did not report about the Fatimids, but about two related movements of more immediate concern for Baghdad and the central territories of the 'Abbasid caliphate, namely the Zanj rebellion among African slave labourers in the marshes of southern Iraq, and the Qarmatians, centred on Bahrain with branches in Iraq and Iran. The leaders of both movements claimed descent from 'Alids in the Isma'ili line. The Qarmatian movement began as a breakout from loyalty with the *Imam*s of the Fatimid line; however, once the Fatimid caliphate was established, all Qarmatians except the Bahrain branch swore loyalty to the Fatimids. (See *Map 2.*)

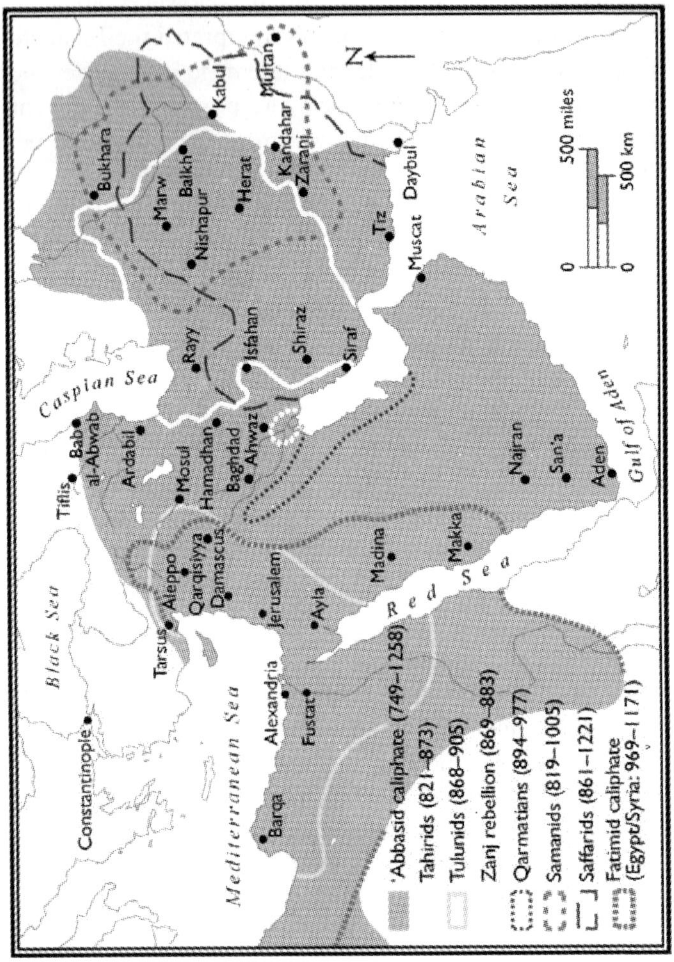

Map 2. *Rebellions and rival dynasties which weakened the power of the 'Abbasid state*

Tabari was vehemently opposed to the Zanj and the Qarmatians. Nevertheless, unlike the Hanbalis, he was not programmatically antagonistic towards the 'Alids as such. He defended their rights just as for any Muslim, as long as they did not rebel against the state. Moreover, while Tabari did not recognize Ibn Hanbal as legal theorist, he had no theoretical issue with the Imami (Ja'fari) school as it was semi-rationalist in the same way as his own Shafi'i school; the Hanbalis in their turn included him in their critique against the Imami Shi'is.

Tabari passed away on the evening of Monday, 27 Shawwal, 310 AH/17 February, 923, at the age of eighty-four. He was buried the morning after in the yard of his own house. According to one report, his last words about his scholarship were: 'My advice for you is to follow my religious practice and to act in accordance with what I have explained in my books' (*History*, i/ Rosenthal. 79).

METHODOLOGY

Tabari produced his works during the third Islamic century when the legal and theological debates of the preceding centuries had crystallized into schools, leaving a considerable legacy of doctrinal works. As noted in the Preface, his five surviving works are major contributions to the disciplines of Prophetic and Companion tradition, jurisprudence, Qur'an commentary, history, and theology. The other works (that we only know of) pertain to those major disciplines, and to related sub-disciplines, such as Arabic language and poetry, the Prophetic biography, ethics, philosophy, and dream interpretation.

The four major works are encyclopaedic in character, as Tabari's basic method was to present as many as possible of the important legal opinions, scriptural interpretations and dogmatic positions, and then set out his own. Thus his works are invaluable summaries of the development of scholarship during the first three Islamic centuries. Since by that time the historical records, traditions and doctrinal works existed in written form, Tabari relied entirely on written sources. It seems he kept working on all his writings more or less at the same time, as they took shape in the form of dictated lectures on specific topics within specific disciplines; hence the recurrent formula 'Abu Ja'far said…' Tabari often referred to his own works in terms of subject-matter, rather than the titles they acquired after they had been formally compiled, e.g. 'my writing on the opinions of the jurists'.

The term 'methodology' refers to the theoretical foundation of a specific method. 'Theory' in its turn requires philosophy. According to the biographical sources, Tabari mastered Greek philosophy, including dialectics and logic. Though he did not devote a specific work to philosophy, it underpinned all his works; in particular, the role of 'reason' as source of knowledge was a consistent reference point. A central issue in Greek philosophy is epistemology or theories about how to acquire knowledge about reality. There are two basic epistemological positions – empiricist and idealist. Empiricists assume that reality consists of material things, and knowledge about reality is gained 'empirically', through sense perceptions of those things. The other, idealist approach is that reality consists of immaterial ideas which correspond to human linguistic concepts, and knowledge about ideas is therefore gained through discursive reasoning, i.e., by thinking rationally about concepts. Tabari represents a synthesis of empiricism and idealism which is expressed in the relative weight he ascribed to empirical 'text' and discursive 'reasoning'. This weight varies, depending on the discipline: for example, theology requires more discursive reasoning than does history, for which knowledge is (typically) dependent on textual records.

The Arabic term for theology is *kalam*, which literally means 'discursive speech'. *Kalam* specifically aimed at gaining knowledge about God. Empiricism in its most pure form is represented by the Hanbalis who, although they produced doctrines about God, cannot be called theologians as they rejected the methodology of *kalam*. God Himself is non-material, they argued, but He has 'revealed' His speech in the form of the Quran, the text which provides an empirical source of knowledge about God. The Prophetic tradition also contains 'revelation', since the Prophet continually received and interpreted God's speech. But beyond these two sets of texts, there is no knowledge about God. Discursive reasoning pertains to the human mind, and to the extent that it claims to produce knowledge about God, it associates humans with God, which is 'idolatry' (*shirk*) and 'unlawful innovation' (*bid'a*). The opposite idealist position and the more properly theological approach is represented by the Mu'tazila, who claimed that since God is non-material, He cannot take material form. The empirical text of the Qur'an is not of God's nature but is a created thing; knowledge about God must therefore derive from discursive speech and reasoning beyond the text.

Tabari's synthesis implied that knowledge about God should be deduced from the Qur'an and the Prophetic tradition by use of reasoning and logic, i.e. departing from the empirical text, but that questions about God could also be formulated independently of the texts. This was similar to the methodology of al-Ash'ari (d. *ca.* 935). Indeed, the Andalusion scholar Ibn Hazm (d. 1064) described Tabari as in line with (but a trifle more radical than) the Ash'ari school, which came to dominate theology in Sunni Islam:

Al-Ṭabarī and all the Ashʿaris, with the exception of al-Samnānī, hold that the exercise of reason is a necessary prerequisite to be a Muslim, without which one is not a Muslim. Al-Ṭabarī declares: 'the man or woman who has reached puberty but ha[s] not yet by way of reasoning (*istidlāl*) learned to know God, together with all

His names and attributes, is an infidel (*kāfir*) {...}.' He also says: 'when the male or female servant [of God] has reached the age of seven, they must be taught and trained in all that.' According to the Ashʿaris, knowing God through reasoning is not required until after puberty.[1]

Theology and epistemology is thus one of the issues which divided Tabari and the Hanbalis. Where the Hanbalis rejected all sources of knowledge about God other than the revealed text and its interpretations by the Prophet, Tabari held that theological discourse was needed precisely because God said *in the revealed text* that He is not material and that humans must exercise reason to know Him. Accordingly, knowledge about God's nature can be sought through reasoning and beyond the empirical text.

Tabari had studied all the schools of law of his time (Hanafi, Maliki, Shafi'i, Zahiri and Ja'fari), although his own jurisprudence followed the Shafi'i school of law. Methodologically, it was characterized by its synthesis of 'revealed text' and 'reasoning', that is, legal rulings were deduced by applying analogical reasoning to the Qur'an and the Prophetic traditions transmitted by the Companions, and the written corpus of the school's previously deduced laws. Through this method, Tabari produced independent legal reasoning which his disciples posthumously called the Jariri school; however, it lasted only one scholarly generation after him. The Shafi'i method also explains why he excluded Ahmad b. Hanbal and the Mu'tazilis from jurisprudence. Ibn Hanbal restricted the textual sources of law to the Qur'an and the Prophetic traditions ('the revealed texts'), rejecting the laws deduced by the jurists; the Mu'tazilis rejected the Prophetic and jurist traditions alike, and deduced legal rulings by

[1] The quotation is from Gilliot, *Exégèse Coranique*, 36, who also cites from the Andalusian theologian Ibn Hazm, *al-Fisal fi l-milal wa-l-ahwa wa-l-nihal*, i. 35, iv. 67.

reasoning from the Qur'an exclusively. Tabari defined jurisprudence as a discipline founded on all categories of textual sources, with deduction as the basic method, and therefore both Ibn Hanbal and the Mu'tazilis failed to meet his minimum requirements.

On a more general level, it is implicit in Tabari's methodology that although empirical perceptions are the only way to know 'the things', the knowledge acquired needs rational thought procedures and discourse to make it intelligible and practicable. That is what his scholarly works were for: to illustrate how knowledge could be made useful.

WORKS

The aim of this section is to provide readers, through a brief overview, with a taste of Tabari's thinking and method in his different works, of which the *History* will be treated at more length in Parts 2 and 3. I have tried to indicate the values and concerns common to the whole corpus.

Sarih al-sunna

In this short treatise Tabari defines his methodology and positions on the major doctrinal debates of his day in relation to the Hanbalis, Mu'tazilis, Qadaris, Murji'is, and Jahmis. We find Tabari mostly in agreement with Ibn Hanbal.

Tabari opens the treatise with the following statement, which illustrates his synthesis between text (here 'tradition') and reason, as well as the practical objective of his scholarly effort, namely to enlighten the ignorant:

> After God's Messenger passed away, he has been followed, in each time and age, by events and calamities which drove the ignorant to seek refuge with the scholar and the scholar to rend the darkness shrouding the ignorant by the knowledge which God had given him as a mark of distinction, partly through tradition

(*āthār*) and partly through reasoning (*naẓar*). (Sourdel, *Profession de foi*, 186[French]/193[Arabic])

Through tradition ('text') and reasoning, then, Tabari defines the issues of dogma, one by one, beginning with the issue of whether the Qur'an is God's eternal word, as the Hanbalis and most others held, or created in time, as the Mu'tazilis and Jahmis proposed. Tabari held that 'the Qur'an is God's word (*kalām Allāh*) and His revelation, and as it consists of a set of ideas (*maʿānī yūṣiduhu*), the correct conclusion is that it is God's uncreated word, however written and wherever recited' (ibid, 187/194). Thus, since God is non-material, the Qur'an can be of Him as the articulation of His eternal, immaterial ideas. Tabari reasoned to this conclusion on the basis of two Qur'anic verses (87. 21–2; 9. 6) and two Companion traditions. The second issue concerned the *ruʾya* or seeing of God in the hereafter. Tabari concluded that the righteous ones who enter Paradise will be able to see God, because that is established by a Prophetic tradition.

The third issue was the famous controversy about whether human acts are predestined by God or freely chosen by humans. The Hanbalis believed in God's absolute power and predestination; the Mu'tazilis favoured the Qadari doctrine of human free will; the Murji'is held that humans exercised free will within certain necessary requirements; and the Jahmis denied any relationship between God and human actions, since only God can act in the true sense of the word. Tabari sides with Ibn Hanbal (and possibly the Murji'is) on this matter, maintaining (again on the basis of a Prophetic tradition) that all acts are 'from God, Who metes them out and effectuates them, so that nothing can come about without His permission and wish; creation is His, and the command'. (Ibid, 189/196)

The fourth issue concerns the merits of the first four Companion caliphs. On the basis of a supporting Prophetic tradition, Tabari affirms that the best among the Companions are Abu Bakr, 'Umar, 'Uthman and 'Ali b. Abi Talib the Commander of the Faithful and Leader (*imam*) of the Pious' (ibid, 190/197). Though this order of merit follows the broad, Sunni ranking of the Companion caliphs, Tabari reserves the title of *imam* for 'Ali, implying a special spiritual rank.

Closely related is the fifth issue, concerning the *imama* or spiritual leadership of the community. Here Tabari cites the Prophetic tradition, transmitted by the Prophet's client Safina:

'The caliphate will be in my community for thirty years, and what comes after that is kingship'. Ṣafina said: 'I added up the caliphates of Abū Bakr, ʿUmar, ʿUthmān and ʿAlī, and it came to thirty years'. (Ibid, 190/197)

Tabari was of the opinion that after the four Companion caliphs there was no longer a caliphate in the sense of *imama*, 'spiritual leadership', only kingship. Here he is in agreement with the Hanbalis, who assigned a special rank to the first four caliphs because of their status as Companions. But it is clear from the *History*, that Tabari did not assign a special rank to them as Companions to the Prophet. It is possible that, for him, the shift from caliphate to kingship refers simply to the historical fact that the end of 'Ali's caliphate entailed a shift in succession, from election on the basis of merit to dynastic rule; hence 'from caliphate to kingship' means 'from election to dynastic succession'.

The sixth issue is faith, whether it consists in confession of belief or deeds, and if it can increase or decrease. Here Tabari relies exclusively on scholarly traditions, since there were no Prophetic or Companion traditions on these matters. The Murji'is and the Jahmis gave primacy to faith as internal knowledge over deeds. The Jahmis also held that since faith is knowledge, it does not decrease even if the person stops believing, because the knowledge is still there; moreover, only God can act in the true sense, and therefore deeds are irrelevant to faith. The Mu'tazilis and the Kharijis, on the other hand, held that faith is necessarily expressed in deeds, and that it both increases and decreases. Tabari followed Ibn Hanbal on the latter issue, holding that faith increases by mentioning and praising God, and decreases by not doing so. On the former issue, he concludes that faith is both belief and deeds, in line with the Mu'tazilis and Ibn Hanbal.

The seventh issue concerns the utterance of the Qur'an: when the faithful utter it, is it then God's word that they utter? Tabari points out that since the debate has arisen recently, guidance must be sought among recent scholars. The main contenders were, again, the Hanbalis, who claimed that the Qur'an is God's uncreated word whether or not it is recited; and the Mu'tazilis and Jahmis who both held that, since the Qur'an as text is created, its utterance pertains to the reader, not to God. Tabari follows Ibn Hanbal, who had stated: 'Those who profess that the pronounced words of the Qur'an are created are Jahmis, for God has said "so that he may hear the word of God" {Q. 9. 6}, among those who had heard it', and 'The one who declares that the words through which he recites the Qur'an are created is a Jahmi, and the one who declares that they are not created is an innovator (*mubtadi*ʕ)' (ibid, 191–2/198). Hence, the words pronounced when someone is reciting the Qur'an are God's eternal words, but they are also created, because they are given sound by a human being.

The last, eighth issue concerns the classical philosophical question of the relationship between the sign (*ism*) and the signified (*musamma*), here applied to God and His attributes. Thus, the question was: is God identical with His attributes? One of the most contended Qur'anic passages was 20. 5–6: 'The Compassionate has seated Himself upon the Throne; to Him belongs what is in the heavens, and what is in the earth, and what is in between them, as well as what is beneath the ground'. The Mu'tazilis and the Jahmis denied identity between God and His attributes, because God is of a nature different from humans, and the attributes describe human characteristics. Verses like the ones above must therefore be read allegorically, as referring to God's power, and not as a description of the human act of 'sitting' on the material thing 'the Throne'. By contrast, the Hanbalis asserted identity between God and His attributes, because God has described Himself in these material terms. Tabari, given the absence of Prophetic traditions on the matter, defers argumentation on it. Instead, he cites two passages from the Qur'an – 'Call on God or the Compassionate. By whatever name you call [Him], His are the Most Beautiful Names' (17. 110), and 'To God belong the Most Beautiful Names, so call Him by them' (7. 180) – which indicate that God identifies Himself with His attributes. Regarding Q. 20. 5–6, Tabari says these verses must be taken as descriptions of God, as must the attributes; thus he avoids allegorical interpretation.

Jami' al-bayan

Tabari's comprehensive Qur'an commentary begins with a methodological introduction, followed by the commentary itself, verse by verse, of the entire Book. Its full Arabic title, *Jāmiʿ al-bayān ʿan taʾwīl āy al-Qurʾān* (hereafter the *Jami'*, which I translate as 'The Comprehensive Collection of Explanations of the Original Meaning of the Signs of the Qur'an'), tells us two things which Tabari explained in his introduction. Firstly, that he collected what he considered to be the most important interpretations of every Qur'anic verse, from the first Muslim generation to his own day. This constitutes the *āthār*, 'tradition', and Tabari's interpretive method was therefore called *tafsīr bi l-maʾthūr*, 'explanation by tradition'. Secondly, the title indicates that Tabari applied a theory of language – it is a means of communicating meaning through signs (*āyāt,* sing. *āya*) – and he applied a corresponding theory of interpretation, according to which interpretation aims at explaining the author's or speaker's intended meaning in a given historical context. Therefore, the most essential knowledge for the interpreter is knowledge of the Arabic language spoken in Makka and Madina at the time of the Prophet, when the Qur'an was revealed, because this was the language that God used to communicate with the Prophet, and through him to his community.

However, to know the meaning communicated in a given historical context, one must also know the speaker because, by Tabari's theory of language, speech always expresses the innermost subjectivity and concerns of the speaker, who seeks to convey these concerns to others:

> Among the greatest blessings which God has conferred upon His servants and the most significant favours He has given to His created beings is the gift of explanation (*bayān*), by which they may give clear expression to their innermost subjects (*ḍamāʾir ṣudūrihim*) and indicate their personal concerns (*ʿaẓāʾim nufūsihim*), for He had by it softened their tongues and eased their difficulties. By it they may pronounce His unity and praise and holiness, and by it they may care for their own needs, converse with each other, get acquainted, and engage with each other. (*Jamiʿ*, i. 16–17; my translation)

The same theory applies to God, Who used language 'signs' (*āyāt*) to communicate His concerns to human communities, through His Messengers, and it is these 'signs' that make up the Qur'an. Since the community to which God addressed the Qur'an spoke Arabic, He used Arabic to communicate with them. The presence of loan words (from Persian, Ethiopian and Aramaic) in the Qur'an does not negate the fact that the language of the Qur'an is Arabic because, Tabari argues, the Arabs at the time had made such foreign (*aʿjam*) words part of their vernacular, and this is reflected in the language God used to communicate with them; but as such words were part of the spoken Arabic of the time, they could no longer be called 'foreign'.

God's Arabic language evinces all the manners of human linguistic expression of the particular time and place. However, there is a crucial difference between God's speech and that of humans, namely that God's speech contains 'the persuasive proof' which He passes on to His Messengers, and which makes people believe that He is the Creator and Judge, who has no equal among His created beings:

Each existing thing testifies to His unity, and each sense-perception is a guide to His lordship, through the characteristics which He made inherent in things, namely shortage and abundance, impotence and need, susceptibility to accidental facts and subjection to inevitable incidents, so that the persuasive proof (*al-ḥujja al-bāligha*) shall belong to Him. Then He arranged the indications testifying to Himself, and in the hearts He established a degree of His splendour to enlighten them, by the Messengers whom He sent to whomsoever He wished of His servants and who called [the people] to the truth that had become clear to them and the proofs that had taken root in their faculties of reasoning, 'so that the people would have no proof against God, once the messengers had come', [Q. 4. 165] and so that He could cause those of discernment and intelligence to remember. He extended His help to [the Messengers] and distinguished them from His other created beings by their ability to give truthful indications of Him, and He supported them in this by [providing them with] the persuasive proofs and the inimitable signs (*al-āy al-muʿjiẓa*), so that no one would be able to say: 'This is, indeed, merely a human being like yourselves, who eats what you eat and drinks what you drink. If you obey a human being like yourselves, you are certain to be losers. [Q. 23. 33–4]' (Ibid, i. 13)

Underlying the first sentence is Tabari's empiricist epistemology: sense-perceptions of existing things are the primary source of knowledge about God, which is then rationalized and 'recognized' in the intellect. What God's speech communicates is that the human experience that all things and creatures are in some way deficient is a proof of the existence of the Creator, Who should be the authoritative guide for all humans. To convince people of this is thus, by implication, God's innermost concern.

The interpreter expresses his innermost concerns and subjectivity too. Since Tabari defines interpretation as 'explaining' through language the meaning of a text, the interpreter, like any speaker, expresses his innermost concerns as he explains the meaning of the text; this is so even when the objective is to explain the other speaker's meaning. This subjective dimension of interpretation is reflected also in Tabari's explanation of the word *qurʾān*. It is a verbal noun from *qaraʾa*, usually rendered as 'to read' or 'recite' but which Tabari said also carries the meaning 'gather together' (*jamaʿa*), and 'join together' (*ḍamma*), because to read is to draw together the ideas in the text. Interpretation (*taʾwīl*) thus involves a twofold 'drawing together of ideas': by reading the ideas contained in the text, and, by explaining them, composing (*taʾlīf*) a new set of ideas, which are the interpreter's interpretation of the text (ibid, i. 65). Tabari demonstrates this throughout the *Jamiʿ*. Through his interpretations, he draws out the meaning-contents of each verse and chooses the relevant exegetical traditions to explain them, be they of philosophical, legal or historical character. Thus, he combined language analysis with contents analysis, making the fullest use of his competence in the other disciplines.

According to Tabari, the Qur'an contains three levels of meaning. The first level cannot be reached by anyone except God, Who has concealed its meaning from all His creatures: it concerns 'the appointed times of the events which will come to pass and which God has described in His writing, such as the Hour of Judgement, Jesus son of Mary's return to earth, the sun's rising in the west, and the sounding of the trumpet', i.e., the events which usher in the end of time and Judgement Day (ibid, i. 64). The second level concerns things which only the Prophet had knowledge about, and which the community can only get to know through his interpretations, i.e. from Prophetic traditions. The third level of meaning is that which only the Arabic speakers at the time of the Prophet knew, and which is contained in the Prophetic and Companion traditions and transmitted from them onwards to the successive generations of interpreters. The first and foremost of the interpreters is 'Abd Allah b. 'Abbas, the Prophet's cousin and ancestor of the 'Abbasid family. Tabari's method is exemplified by his commentary on Qur'an 3. 5–7, where he explains what 'the first level of meaning' is and why its meaning is known only to God:

It is [God] Who has sent down to you the written document (*kitāb*),[1] with signs which are precise in meaning (*āyāt muḥkamāt*), and which are its substance, and others which are ambiguous (*mutashābihāt*). As for those whose hearts are devious, they follow the ambiguous [signs], seeking dissent as they seek to interpret them. However, no one knows how to interpret them except God. Those of profound scholarship say: 'We believe in it, for it is all from our Lord'; but it is only the discerning scholars who keep this in mind. (Q. 3. 5–7)

Tabari begins by giving his own explanations of the verses, and then backing these up with Prophetic and Companion traditions, many from Ibn 'Abbas. He systematically explains the meaning of each sentence, and then sums up in a paraphrase of verse 3. 5 as follows:

Therefore the interpretation of the words is as follows: It is He from whom nothing on the earth or in the heavens is concealed Who has sent down to you, O Muḥammad, the Qur'an. It contains signs that can be precisely explained, which are the foundation of the writing and the religious support of you and your community, and the refuge for you and them concerning the rules of Islam which are incumbent upon you all; and it contains other signs which are ambiguous as to how they should be recited, and which have several possible meanings. (*Jami'*, iii. 233–4)

---

[1] I have preferred to translate *kitāb* as 'written document' (rather than 'the Book'), in line with the same preference later in the argument: see below pp. 49ff., 119, 135, 149.

Then Tabari proceeds to give the different interpretations of the same verse. For example, one group among the Companions (including Ibn 'Abbas) argued that the *muḥkamāt* were later verses which abrogated earlier ones, and that therefore the *mutashābihāt* were the abrogated verses; others held the *muḥkamāt* to be the stories and reports in which God passed judgement on the peoples and Messengers, whom He distinguished from Muhammad and his people, whereas the *mutashābihāt* are verses that can be applied to several different peoples.

Tabari instead interprets *mutashābihāt* as signs with several different meanings. He refers to other Companions who interpreted the term as referring to two things, both of which signify 'ambiguity': the events signalling the end times, and the inexplicable disjunct letters which introduce certain Qur'anic chapters. These Companions claimed that the verse was revealed when a group of Jews in Madina, wanting to know when the rule of Islam would come to an end and hoping they might be able to work out what the signs of the end would be, thought that the disjunct letters held an explanation. But God revealed to them and the Muslims that only He knows these things; that it is futile for humans to speculate about them; instead, they should abide by the religious commandments until Judgement Day. Another group of Companions held that it was a group of Christians from Najran who came to discuss with the Prophet the meaning of Jesus being the Holy Spirit. A third interpretation by the Companion Qatada was that the verse refers to groups of Muslims (in the future), the Kharijis and the Saba'is, one extremist Sunni and one proto-Isma'ili movement, who played important parts in furthering the schism between Sunni and Shi'i Islam:

[A]bout [God's] words 'As for those whose hearts are devious, they follow the ambiguous [signs], seeking dissent as they seek to interpret them'. When Qatada read 'those whose hearts are devious' he said: 'If those are not the Kharijis and the Saba'is, then I don't know who they could be! By my life, in the people of Badr and Hudaybiyya who witnessed, together with God's Messenger, the oath of allegiance sworn by the content Emigrants and Helpers, there is information for those who want to be informed and admonition for those who wish to be admonished, for those who reflected or observed. The Kharijis left (*kharajū*) at a time when the Companions of God's Messenger were many in Madina and Syria and Iraq, and when his wives were still alive and, by God, not one single man or woman of them 'left'. But [the Kharijis] were not content with what they had and did not help the others, and instead they said shameful things about God's Messenger and described him in bad ways, for they hated them in their hearts and vilified them with their tongues and by God, their power grew stronger against their group. By my life, if the command of the Kharijis was divine guidance, they would have united, but they were in error and therefore they split up; that is how one knows when something is not from God: it is full of contentious differences [...]. Theirs is a bad religion so keep away from it. By God, the Jewish religion is innovation (*bidʿa*), the Christian religion is innovation, the Khariji religion is innovation, and the Saba'i religion is innovation: no writing has come down to them and they do not have a prophet as model. (Ibid, 242–3)

It is clear that Qatada's concerns as interpreter were the Kharijis and the Saba'is, whom he perceived as a great menace, and whom he thought could be included in the general significance of the verse 3. 7. However, the Kharijis and the Saba'is were much later than the verse. Therefore, to avoid anachronism he put them on a par with the Jews and the Christians of the Prophet's time. Tabari seems to have accepted Qatada's approach, because he too interpreted the verse as referring to 'the innovators', or those who introduced new beliefs in Islam, especially such as associated man with the divine (*shirk*), for example by claiming knowledge about the end times:

Provided that this sign was revealed concerning those we think, namely those who associate others with God (*ahl al-shirk*), its meaning applies to everyone who introduces new beliefs in God's religion and whose heart is inclined to such things, so that he interprets some of the ambiguous signs of the Qur'an and then uses dialectics to prove the truth of his interpretation against those who adhere to the truth, and diverts the faithful seekers of truth from the clarity of the precise signs to confusion, as he claims knowledge to interpret the ambiguous. This can concern anyone and any form of innovation, be it Christianity, or Judaism, or Zoroastrianism, or the Saba'is, or Kharijis, or Qadaris, or Jahmis; as [the Prophet] said: 'When you come across those who use dialectics, they are the ones whom God meant, so beware of them.' (Ibid, 246)[1]

Thus, to seek to interpret the 'ambiguous signs' equals the first level of interpretation, i.e. about the end times, which only God knows; and since there are no clear texts about this, the only way to try to get knowledge about it is through 'dialectical discoursing'. In the *History*, Tabari gives an example of such 'dialectical discoursing' by Qarmat, founder of the revolutionary Qarmatian movement. Here Tabari describes how he campaigned to attract followers for his planned war against the 'Abbasid state:

Settling in a place known as al-Nahrayn, he led an ascetic life and displayed his piety to all. He earned his living by weaving baskets from palm leaves, and spent much of his time praying. He continued this way for some time. If anyone joined him, he would discourse with him upon religious affairs, inculcate him with contempt for this world, and teach him that it was incumbent upon everyone to pray fifty times each day and night. He did this until news spread about his activity in this place. Then he disclosed that he was urging allegiance to an Imām from the house of the Messenger. He went on in this manner attracting people to his side and spreading his message which won over their hearts. (*History*, xxxvii/Fields. 169–70)

Tabari did not himself directly describe Isma'ili interpretation, but two examples from early Fatimid sources will give

---

[1] The Prophetic tradition mentioned is from the *Sunan* of Ibn Maja, Introduction to Chapter (*bāb*) 7.

the reader an idea of what it was about. The first is from the propaganda about the returning *Imam* and imminent end of the ʻAbbasid caliphate, paving the way for Fatimid rule. Written by the Fatimid chief judge, al-Qadi al-Nuʻman, it illustrates how Ismaʻili propaganda appropriated God's knowledge of the signs of the end-times to portend the fall of the ʻAbbasids:

The governors of the ʻAbbasids are twenty governors,
The lands of the west obey them against their will,
But in ninety-six a banner will come down [...]
The sun of God will rise from the West [...]
From the sons of Fatima will come forth a man [...]
He will fill God's earth with justice and mercy,
With days of sincerity and beneficial attainments,
But by the one-eyed Deceiver (*al-Dajjāl*) his assembled legions will be demolished,
Except for a band rising in the mountain high and stable.
Then Jesus son of Mary will slay (the Deceiver),
With the power of a Lord who has no conqueror.
Then the son of Mary will die, returning to God [...]
(Haji, *Fatimid State*, 68)

The second example is from *Kitab al-Munazarat* ('The Book of Debates'), by Ibn al-Haytham, the tenth-century Fatimid scholar-propagandist from Qayrawan (Tunisia). It illustrates how Ismaʻili interpreters departed from the linguistic-historical meaning of the text, in order to make it signify what was in line with their Ismaʻili-Shiʻi concerns:

I said: [...] Most of the religion consists of allusion and parables, and this is explanation and clarification. Hence, we are able to declare that ʿAlī b. Abī Ṭālib is the person designated for the Imamate following the Apostle of God on the basis of God, the Most High, having said: 'In the mother of the Book which is with Us, he is ʿAlī, full of wisdom' (Q. 43:4); and God's statement, 'We appointed for them ʿAlī as a voice of truth' (Q. 19:50); and His statement, 'This is the straight path of ʿAlī' (Q. 15:41). For the person of intelligence, the indication given in these phrases is enough and does not need to be clarified or explained.

[The opponent] said: The specialists in language would preclude your saying this and would oppose you in what you intend by it. Grammatical rules do not allow what you claim on behalf of ʿAlī or that he is meant by *ʿaliyyan* or that he is *ʿaliyyun*, full of wisdom; and moreover, there were in the family other scholars of perfect knowledge such as ʿAbdallāh b. ʿAbbās.
I said: As for the freedmen and their sons, they have no share in the Imamate nor any portion of it and no priority in Islam or in jihad on behalf of God. All of this, however, is combined in ʿAlī. The rules of grammar are whatever conveys the truth. The nominative and genitive consist in whatever puts it in the proper places with sound meanings in accordance with the intention of God, the Mighty and Glorious, and thus the nominative is for His friends and the genitive is for His enemies. These people claim to be reading the letters of the language correctly grammatically, and yet they are ignorant of what God, the Mighty and Glorious, intended in regard to meanings, applications, and examples. The allusions, symbols, and implications are God's, the Mighty and Glorious, and only those possessing knowledge will comprehend them. (Madelung and Walker, *The Advent*, 85–6)

In theology, Tabari allowed reasoning beyond the text, but not in interpretation. Here his empiricist methodology, focused on language and historical information, contrasts sharply with the Isma'ili idealist approach, in which discursive reasoning (as Tabari would see it) transgresses the proper boundaries of linguistic-historical analysis. Politically, Tabari's empiricism is on the side of the state and aspires to reform its administration, while the Isma'ili idealism is subversive of the established interpretative traditions loyal to the state.

My last examples from the *Jami'* bring us back again to language. They concern the famous 'seven readings' of the Qur'an, and the collection of the standard text by the third Companion caliph, 'Uthman b. 'Affan (r. 644–56). Having demonstrated that God sent down the Qur'an in Arabic (since the 'foreign' words had been assimilated into the Arabs' regular usage), Tabari asked *which* Arabic it was that the Qur'an was revealed in, since there were many different dialects. Was it one of these, or a hybrid of them all? Since

God had not said anything about this, the only way to know was through the Prophet:

The Prophet said: 'The Qur'an was sent down on seven letters (*ʿalā sabʿat aḥruf*), and disputation over the Qur'an is unbelief (*kufr*)' – and this he repeated three times – 'so act according to what you have understood from it, and that which you do not understand you should refer to those who are knowledgeable.' (*Jami'*, i. 24–5)[1]

Then Tabari cites numerous Prophetic and Companion traditions to show that even during the Prophet's lifetime, the Companions read the Qur'an differently, and that the tradition about the Qur'an having been sent down 'on seven letters' could mean either seven different pronunciations or seven kinds of addresses – namely, injunctions, reprimands, exhortations, warnings, stories, allegories, and the like. Tabari settled for the interpretation that 'seven letters' meant seven (or more) pronunciations, because this was what the reliable traditions from the Prophet said: the Companions read the Qur'an differently, and disagreed over how it should be read, and the different readings came to be identified with different Companions.

Tabari leads this topic over to the issue of the writing down and 'canonizing' of the Qur'an. After the Prophet's death, many Companions were killed in battles against renegade tribes during the caliphate of Abu Bakr (r. 632–34). 'Umar b. al-Khattab suggested that since the Qur'an was contained in the Companions' memories, it was best to write it down lest knowledge of it was lost with their deaths. This was done by the Prophet's scribe Zayd b. Thabit. However, during the caliphate of 'Uthman, it became evident that the people of the different provinces were still reading the Qur'an according to the different readings mentioned

---

[1] The Prophetic tradition is from Ibn Hanbal, *al-Musnad*, no. 7995, in vol. 3 of the Dar al-Fikr edition.

above, and therefore ʿUthman decided to produce one canonical text, which would be distributed to all the provinces. This was how the *muṣḥaf* (lit. 'the collection of pages', or 'the copy') came about.

Tahdhib al-athar

Another major work is *Kitāb Tahdhīb al-āthār wa tafsīl maʿānī al-thābit ʿan Rasūl Allāh min al-akhbār* ('Refinement of the Traditions and Detailed Exposition of the Meaning of Reliable Reports from God's Messenger'), hereafter *Tahdhib*. Tabari might have started this work with *al-Musnad* in mind, Ibn Hanbal's vast collection of Prophetic and Companion traditions. Ibn Hanbal's compilation sought to provide an 'empirical', textual corpus of traditions from the Prophet's generation, when divine guidance was immediate. The choice of title (*Musnad*) indicates that Ibn Hanbal did not arrange the traditions thematically but according to the *isnād*s, or the chains of transmitting authorities; e.g., listing the traditions transmitted by the Companion caliphs: first Abu Bakr, then ʿUmar, then ʿUthman, then ʿAli. However, the *Musnad* does not provide any analysis of the contents of the traditions. Tabari's contribution in the *Tahdhib* was to provide, in Rosenthal's words, 'an exhaustive and penetrating analysis of the philological and legal implications of each *ḥadīth* mentioned and to discuss its meaning as well as its significance for religious practice and theory' (*History*, i/ Rosenthal. 128). The *Tahdhib* is arranged as a *musnad*, i.e. under the name of the Companion who reported them from the Prophet. For example, *Musnad ʿAli* (the part of the book edited by Mahmud Muhammad Shakir) compiles the Prophet's traditions reported by his cousin ʿAli. However, within that arrangement, Tabari has organized the traditions thematically, so that they could serve as commentaries and rulings on specific legal and theological issues. His method is to begin by citing one Prophetic tradition on a specific legal issue; then the different versions of it with evaluation of the transmitting authorities; other Prophetic traditions on related subjects; linguistic analysis (often by referring to poetry) to determine the precise meaning of the tradition; and after all that, he defines his own position on the issue and describes its broader significance. In the course of determining significance, he produced substantial legal and theological treatises.

Kitab Ikhtilaf

Tabari used the same basic method in *Kitāb Ikhtilāf ʿulamāʾ al-amṣār fī sharāʾiʿ al-islām* ('The Book on the Differences of Opinion among the Scholars of the Metropolises Regarding the Rulings of Islam', hereafter *Ikhtilaf*). It is in this work that Tabari famously offended the Hanbalis by not including Ibn Hanbal. As the title indicates, the purpose of *Ikhtilaf* was to define points of disagreement among jurists. It is an early example of a genre that became established over the centuries after Tabari. In contrast to the *Tahdhib*, the *Ikhtilaf* was arranged thematically, by legal topic. The volume of Arabic text edited by Friedrich Kern (1902) includes *Kitab al-Mudabbar* ('Treatise on the Manumitted Slave'), on conditions for freeing a slave upon his owner's death, and *al-Mazaraʿa wa-l-masaqa* ('Sowing and Irrigation') on, among other things, conditions for hiring farming labour; and *Kitab al-Ghasb* ('Treatise on Unlawful Appropriation').

Kitab al-Jihad, Tabari's treatise on 'just war' is available in a recent English translation by Yasir Ibrahim, based on an Istanbul manuscript which Kern never had time to edit. Given contemporary concerns on the issue, it is worth noting that for the jurists whose arguments Tabari presents, *jihad* was a matter for the state, *not* individuals, and it was legitimate only in the context of presumed hostility by a non-Muslim state. (See Ibrahim, *Book of Jihad*, 41.)

Tabari's method in the *Ikhtilaf* is to begin by defining the legal issue and giving his own analysis of the legal principles involved. Then he cites the founders of the legal schools (e.g., Abu Hanifa, al-Shafi'i, Malik b. Anas and al-Awza'i) and their principal disciples, focusing on points of disagreement and weaknesses in the arguments, as well as looking at which Qur'anic verses and Prophetic traditions they depended upon, and assessing the reliability of those traditions; finally, he arrives at his own conclusion as to which of the cited opinions are sound. However, he does not offer independent judgements in the *Ikhtilaf*, as the genre is dedicated to describing points of disagreement. It is in a supplement to the *Ikhtilaf* titled *al-Latif fi ahkam shara'i' al-islam* ('The Digest of the Shari'a Rulings of Islam'), that he presents a systematic exposition of the legal principles and their related cases, and his own judgements. This text became the foundation of the short-lived Jariri school.

The History

The subject-matter of *Ta'rikh al-rusul wa-l-muluk* ('The History of the Messengers and the Kings') is Persian, Israelite and Arab kingdoms and prophets, from the creation of the world to the 'Abbasid caliphate until 915. Self-evidently, this is a stretch of time difficult to define; Tabari certainly found it a problem. There were so many conflicting calendars in existence for the period of antiquity, he could not present a coherent chronology until the beginning of the Islamic calendar in 622. His solution was to begin the *History* with the Biblical creation myth, suitably Islamized. The total amount of time, from creation to Judgement Day, he concluded, was seven thousand years, which left his contemporaries with about two hundred years to go. Then he used the Persian king lists as the backbone into which reports about the Israelite and Arab 'messengers and kings' were woven. These king lists were put together from the Sassanid (226–651) chronicles and the Zoroastrian Avesta. The Avesta is in its turn notoriously hard to date; some material may date as far back as the Medic kingdom (sixth century BC), some to the Achaemenid dynasty (559–330 BC), and some to the Sassanids. Using Persian king lists as a frame of reference had some side-effects on the chronology. The earliest possibly 'real' history (as opposed to myth) which Tabari treats seems to be the Israelite kingdom of David, around the turn of the century 1000/900 BC. However, because he took the Persian king lists as point of departure, the section on David in the *History* comes after narratives about Persian kings which were from much later periods. But, chronological complexities aside, with the historical king David as starting point and the 'Abbasid caliphate in 915 as the end, Tabari's *History* spans almost 1800 years.

In Tabari's other main works, he always clearly states his own positions and interpretations. Not so in the *History*. However, according to his own theory that speech expresses the speaker's innermost, subjective concerns, it can be no exception. Thus, while he does not explicitly state his personal opinions about historical events, they are expressed in other forms. The title's 'messengers and kings' tells us that he conceived of history as a succession of religious institutions ('messengers') and states ('kings'), with Islam and the caliphate as direct continuations of the region's religious and monarchic legacies. It is also interesting to note, given Tabaristan's Sassanid heritage, that Tabari provided rich information about the Persian dynasties, and made the Islamic state appear as a legitimate successor to the Sassanid empire. He also paid attention to political developments in and around Tabaristan. These and other signs of Tabari's own hand at work indicate that the entire

History expresses Tabari's 'concerns' in the broader sense, including methodology and analytical concepts.

In spite of this, only a couple of studies have attempted to treat the whole *History*. One of the reasons might be its form. Modern academic historical writing is done as a coherent narrative in which the historian presents readers with his or her analysis, and subordinates primary and secondary sources to the first person voice through the apparatus of footnotes. Tabari's *History* is composed in a form peculiar to early Islamic historical writing, the so-called *khabar* (pl. *akhbār*), literally 'a piece of information.' A *khabar* consists of two parts: (1) a chain of authorities (*isnād*), from a witness of the event to the writing historian, who have passed on the information; and then (2) the information itself. The *khabar* is thus the source moved from footnote to main text. Sometimes the same event is reported differently by different historical authorities, because they assign different significance to it, or pay attention to some aspect of it which others ignore or consider less important; hence, as a rule, reports will be found to agree on basic facts, but differ over details. The multitude of reports on the same topic conveys the impression that the author resides in the background, and is merely presenting source material. Tabari generally reported different versions, provided he found them to be authentic, making only sparse comments on their reliability. Studies of specific historical events and the way in which Tabari pieced together and commented on *akhbār* have shown that it is precisely by looking at his arrangement of reports that we can find his own opinions. (See Further Reading.) Marshall Hodgson (1968) in particular observed that Tabari's reports about the war between 'Ali and Mu'awiya over the caliphate show his concern to develop a law that would, among other things, regulate succession so as to prevent civil strife. Hodgson did not follow up his observation. This book is an attempt to do so, relating Tabari's concern for 'rule of law' to the concepts 'covenant' (*mīthāq*) and 'contract' (*ʿahd*).

Another and related problem in understanding the *History* concerns its 'religious' accent and contents. In the Introduction, Tabari described God as Creator and ultimate cause of history, and throughout the *History*, there are innumerable references to the Qur'an and the Prophetic traditions. Thus, the *History* has been described as founded on a God-centred worldview, to the effect that Tabari analysed history only in terms of individuals' morality and ethically motivated choices which, however, ultimately followed the destinies God had already set for them. This is at odds with modern history, which elevates human autonomy to centre stage, and analyses human actions according to modern theories of society as constituted by several independent spheres – state, law, economy, professions, and so on. In contrast, Tabari and medieval Islamic historians are said to have conceived of society as a hierarchic, organic whole with God's deputy, the caliph, at its apex; because of the organic view of society, the social whole was assumed to be dependent on the ruler's actions, rather than on complex interactions between different social spheres. (See Further Reading.) In this book, I argue that Tabari conceived of society as constituted by distinct spheres and groups, and that his central concern as historian was how the law should serve these different spheres and groups in the most rational way. From this viewpoint, God symbolizes the principle of the rationality of the state law, rather than legitimizing a particular organization of society. This implies that, for Tabari, the only immutable truth is the principle that society needs rule of law, while different societies and their positive laws are subject to change.

Part 2

Reading the *History*

In this part of the book, I will describe the society Tabari dealt with in his *History* in order to pinpoint his personal concerns.

THE SYSTEM OF VASSALAGE

The societies of Mesopotamia, the heartlands of the ‘Abbasid caliphate, had been agrarian since ancient times. Land was the foremost form of property and source of wealth, agriculture being the main economically productive activity generating most of traded goods. Tax on land and agricultural produce was accordingly the main source of income for the state. By the time of the late Sassanid empire, the imperial domains were so vast that the central state's army alone could not control them. The state depended on vassal kings in the provinces to raise armies and defend their part of the imperial territories. In legal theory, the king (Persian, *shāh*) was the sole owner of land, which he assigned to his vassals. The vassals possessed the land in every important sense, including the right to sell it. However, the Shah's legal status as the sole owner of land gave him the right to withdraw assignments from any vassal who did not fulfil his obligations to the state. In the system of vassalage as it worked in practice, this was the state's only counter-measure against the recurrent problem of vassals becoming disloyal and setting up as rivals to state power. Taxation of assigned land and agricultural produce was the main source of income for everyone. The vassals taxed the peasants working their lands, and were allowed to keep some for themselves, and pay the rest to the state treasury. The state needed revenue from the vassals and its 'crown lands' to pay its military to balance the power of the vassals. Other interest groups were the civil administration, the religious institutions and the peasants. It was almost always a problem to make land tax revenue suffice for all social groups without literally killing the peasants in the process.[1]

A specific piece of land had provided a significant part of the agricultural produce and land tax for Mesopotamian empires, namely the Sawad. The name means 'the black soil' and refers to the rich plains between the Euphrates and the Tigris. Under the Sassanids, parts of the Sawad were crown lands, meaning that the Shah had assigned them to other members of the Sassanid royal house. Other parts were assigned to Zoroastrian fire temples and to Nestorian Christian churches; Zoroastrianism and Nestorianism were the two religious communities linked to the Sassanian royal family, but other religious communities were present in the empire, notably Jews and Christians of other creeds. The religious institutions were assigned their lands as a return for collecting tax from their communities' peasants for the state treasury.

After the Arab-Muslim forces defeated the Sassanids in 636–7, the caliph, 'Umar b. al-Khattab (r. 634–44), distributed lands in the Sawad to the conquering commanders and forces, including the right to tax the resident tenant farmers,

---

[1] See Abbas Vali, *Pre-capitalist Iran*, 162–92.

most of whom were then Jews and Christians. In a later legal treatise, *Kitab al-Kharaj* ('The Book on Land Tax'), the Hanafi jurist Abu Yusuf (d. 795) reported that 'Umar at some point stopped doing that and instead turned parts of the Sawad into state-administered lands, as they had been under Sassanid rule. The reason given for this change in policy was the need to pay the military and to meet other needs. The measure was agreed by 'Uthman and 'Ali, his successors.[1]

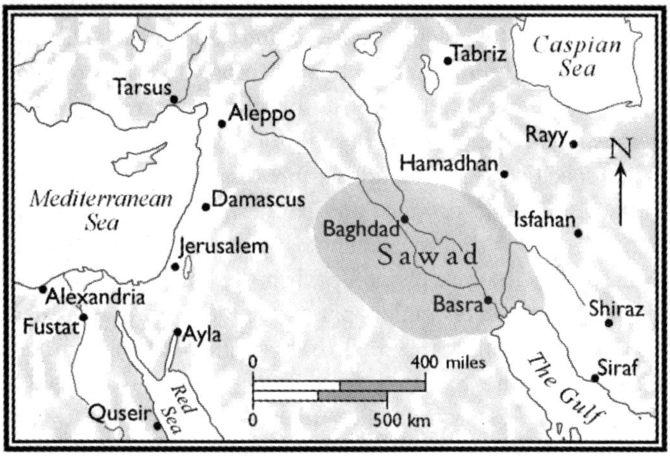

Map 3. *The Sawad*

Between the late seventh and the mid-ninth century, the caliphate was able to go on enlarging its territory through military campaigns and pay a growing civil state administration. In the Arabian Peninsula, particularly its western region of Hijaz, there were rich reserves of gold, silver and copper providing bullion for a powerful currency, which boosted trade and brought in vast income for the state, additional to land tax revenue. However, although mining in the Hijaz continued until at least the eleventh century, the commercial

[1]See Ben Shemesh, *Taxation in Islam*, 70–80.

economy had long since peaked.[1] By Tabari's time, the 'Abbasid state was left with a huge territory to govern, a large military, and an extensive civil administration in place mainly to prevent the military from plundering the peasants but ironically only adding to their tax burden as it too was paid for from land tax revenue. Overtaxed peasants joined rebellions or simply deserted their farmlands, which diminished land tax revenue. The Isma'ili-led rebellions (for example, the Qarmatians and especially the Zanj), which erupted in the central caliphate in the late ninth century, recruited followers among the desperate peasants and agricultural slave workers. The rebels also robbed caravans and disrupted trade routes, exacerbating the decline. In the northern and eastern parts of the empire, vassals established themselves as independent rulers and withheld tax revenue.

The central government was also losing its military autonomy in relation to the vassals. When the 'Abbasids came to power in 749–50, their state army was composed of Arab tribal fighters and troops from Khurasan, a province in western Iran in which the 'Abbasids had a support base. However, from the 840s onwards, the state army was transformed into a praetorian guard, made up of slave soldiers from the caliphate's border regions, and increasingly of Turkish origin. The idea was that soldiers without ties to regional tribes and vassal families would be loyal to the caliph. But their loyalty depended on payment. As long as they were paid from the state treasury, their loyalty was secure. However, as state finances declined they had to be paid by assigning lands to their commanders, which again shifted loyalties away from the state.

---

[1] Heck, 'Gold Mining in Arabia', 370, 385.

THE 'ABBASID ADMINISTRATION

In the 'Abbasid caliphate, the caliph presided over the court of grievances (*maẓālim*) and functioned as commander-in-chief (*amīr al-muʾminīn*), while the state administration was headed by the vizier, or 'prime minister', who directed the state treasury and finances, including payment of the military, and the state departments and their staff, the scribes (*kātib*, pl. *kuttāb*). The administration had laws (*qānūn*) which partly overlapped with the Shari'a; land tax (*kharāj*) was one of them. It was largely the viziers and scribes who were responsible for the problems of balancing the state budget and managing the empire.

The caliph al-Mahdi (r. 775–85) instituted a system called *muqāsama*, which meant that the vassal determined the land tax case by case, according to water supply, area of cultivation, and size of harvest. The advantage from the peasants' point of view was that tax could be reduced if conditions were unfavourable. The disadvantage for peasants was that they were at the mercy of the vassal who was in practice free to ignore circumstances, and for the state that the vassals often withheld the tax revenue due. After the commercial economy peaked in the second half of the ninth century, administrators were divided between those who favoured military expansion above all and therefore subordinated commercial activities to the military need for tax, and those who wanted the military to be defensive rather than expansive, and therefore favoured a moderate taxation of peasants and encouraging commerce outside the control of military commanders.[1]

The period 870–908 saw a brief revival of state power under the caliphs al-Mu'tamid (r. 870–92), al-Mu'tadid (892–

---

[1] Von Sivers, 'Taxes and Trade', 81–5.

902), and al-Muktafi (902–08).[1] During this period, two parties of scribes had crystallized within the administration around two families, Banu al-Furat and Banu al-Jarrah. Banu al-Furat were a successful merchant family whose policy was to extract as much tax revenue as possible from the Sawad and its peasants. It seems that they also separated the financing of the civil administration and the military, using tax revenue to pay the former while letting the military pay itself from its commanders' lands. Opposed to them was a group of scribal families with roots in the Sawad countryside, and of Nestorian Christian origins, who clearly favoured a 'defensive' military posture. Among them were Banu al-Jarrah, who were closely aligned to the military. Their policy is illustrated by al-Mu'tamid's vizier 'Ubayd Allah b. Yahya b. al-Khaqan (d. 877, the one who appointed Tabari as tutor for his son Muhammad). He secured the loyalty of the caliph's troops by having them paid from the state treasury rather than by their tribal commanders. This balancing of the state's tax revenue between military and civil administration was typical of Banu al-Jarrah.

The rivalry between these two families came to the fore most forcefully under the reign (908–32) of the boy caliph al-Muqtadir, about the time that Tabari was finishing the *History*. This reign marks the transition from the brief revival of state power to irreversible decline. His first vizier was Ibn al-Furat who held the vizierate in three periods (908–12, 917–18, 923–4), interspersed by Tabari's former student, Muhammad b. 'Ubayd Allah b. al-Khaqan (912–13), then 'Ali b. 'Isa of Banu al-Jarrah (913–17), and finally the merchant Hamid b. al-'Abbas (918–23). Ibn al-Furat's first period (908–12) was characterized by the appointment of family, friends, and clients to attractive posts, and raising the 'Abbasid family's allowances. Eventually these expenditures

---

[1] See Kennedy, *The Prophet*, 175.

led to his downfall as he emptied the state treasury and had to start taking from the caliphs' fund to cover the deficit. He was succeeded first by Tabari's student Ibn al-Khaqan, who was allied with Banu al-Jarrah but did a very poor job, putting on the payroll more or less everyone who wanted to be on it.[1] Banu al-Jarrah and the caliph's court had him replaced by 'Ali b. 'Isa b. al-Jarrah, one of their kin.

'Ali b. 'Isa has come down in history as 'the good vizier': righteous, austere, and intent on balancing the budget in order to strengthen the state. He put an end to war campaigns against both the Byzantines and the Isma'ilis (Qarmatians and Fatimids), offering instead peace treaties and financial settlements. Similarly, he never exacted vengeance on personal enemies, as was customary in the administration. He had the Baghdad military commander Mu'nis as his personal ally, and made sure the military was paid from the state treasury on a regular basis. Part of financing the military came from cutbacks on court and administrative expenditures, including the 'Abbasids' allowances.

Significant for this exposition of Tabari's *History* are some tax reforms 'Ali b. 'Isa instituted. The province of Fars had been one of the most important farming regions, yielding a large portion of the caliphate's tax revenue. In 869 it was conquered by the Saffarid dynasty, based in Sistan, who recognized the 'Abbasid caliphs only formally. To finance their conquests, the Saffarids instituted a *muqāsama* tax system so extortionate that many farmers fled their lands, which the ones who remained had to pay for by an additional tax. From 900 on the Saffarids were pushed back by the Samanids. Ibn al-Furat took advantage of this to bring Fars back under 'Abbasid state control. He kept both the *muqāsama* system and the additional tax imposed by the Saffarids, which meant that farmers continued to abandon

---

[1] Sourdel, *Le Vizirat 'Abbaside*, (1960) ii. 398.

their lands. When 'Ali b. 'Isa succeded Ibn al-Furat, he abolished the additional tax, and shifted levying and collecting of tax from the vassals to the state administration and his own control. The additional tax was replaced by a tax on fruit trees, said to have been an ancient local tax abolished when the caliph al-Mahdi instituted the *muqasama*. In this way, farmers would not be taxed more than they could cope with, which would keep them on their lands, in turn yielding a much larger tax revenue for the state. In spite of successes in balancing the budget and securing the army, 'Ali b. 'Isa's financial restrictions on the court and civil administration made him enemies, who eventually had him deposed and replaced by Ibn al-Furat. 'Ali b. 'Isa made one come-back to the vizierate, but in 923 (the year of Tabari's death), he was again replaced by Ibn al-Furat. From the viewpoint of the 'Abbasid administration, the road from there was one long unbroken decline, until the Buyids in 945 established themselves as Shahs in Baghdad, alongside the 'Abbasid caliphs.[1]

Tabari as jurist and historian of the caliphate would have been familiar with the problems facing the 'Abbasid state and administration. 'Ali b. 'Isa is barely mentioned in Tabari's *History*, and nothing is said about his policies (*History*, 38/Rosenthal. 80, 118, 199, 204). However, they were acquainted. The vizier, who was unfavourably disposed towards the Hanbalis, once arranged a debate between Tabari and his Hanbali opponents on the interpretation of the Qur'anic verse 17. 78, but only Tabari showed up. 'Ali b. 'Isa also took a personal interest in Tabari's health, sending a physician to him when he had heard that he was ill. In this book I will be arguing that Tabari sided with Banu al-Jarrah and 'Ali b. 'Isa, whose policies, including the centralized tax

---

[1] On the restoration and the scribal families, see Kennedy, *The Prophet*, 175–89; on 'Ali b. 'Isa, see Sourdel, *Le Vizirat 'Abbaside*, 388–422; Bowen, *The Good Vizier*, 99–222.

system, he considered to be rational government and the key to imperial power.

'COVENANT', CONTRACT, AND PROMISED LAND

Before turning to the *History* proper, it will be worthwhile to look at certain concepts which occur throughout Tabari's works, and which may be related to the system of vassalage. These are derived from the Qur'an, where their usage is explicitly linked by Tabari to their Biblical equivalents. The Qur'anic Arabic concepts are *mīthāq*, commonly translated as 'covenant' (e.g.: Q. 2. 83; 3. 81; 4. 90; 5. 12; 7. 169; 13. 20); *ʿahd*, often also rendered as 'covenant' or 'contract' (e.g.: Q. 13. 20; 7. 134; 43. 49; 2. 125; 36. 60); and *arḍ*, or 'land'. The Biblical Hebrew equivalents are *berit*, 'covenant', *tôrah*, 'law', and *eretz*, 'land'.

In particular 'covenant' needs to be explored further, if we are to understand its significance in Tabari's works. In ordinary usage, 'covenant' refers to the pact which God in the Hebrew Bible entered with, first, Noah, then the Patriarchs, then Moses, and finally with the Kings; in the Christian New Testament, Christ represents a new covenant between God and humans. Basically, the covenant defines how God wants to be worshiped, and what He gives in return for right worship. A recurrent Biblical theme is the accusation, voiced mainly by the prophets, that people or kings have violated the covenant by worshiping God in the wrong way: in the Hebrew Bible, by worshiping other gods in the image of humans; in the New Testament, by worshiping him according to Moses' *tôrah*. The Qur'an contains the same concept of covenant, expressed in the two terms *mīthāq* and *ʿahd*, and levels the same accusations but now directed against both Jews and Christians, namely for worshiping humans instead of God (e.g. Q. 9. 31: 'They take their rabbis and monks as lords besides God, as well as the Messiah, son of Mary, although they are commanded to worship none but One God. There is no god but He; exalted is He above what they associated with him').

So far, 'covenant' appears to relate to an entirely religious concern with correct worship of God. In Tabari's *History*, however, the terms *mīthāq* and *ʿahd* are sometimes used in secular contexts, referring to contracts between people. In the *Jami*ʿ, Tabari explains Q. 7. 169: 'Are they not bound by the covenant of the written document (*mīthāq al-kitāb*) […]?'[1] by referring to the Israelites' Biblical covenant as expressed in Moses' *tôrah*, thus explicitly linking the Qur'anic concepts with those of the Hebrew Bible:

Here God said: Those who take bribes when they make judgements, and who say [to themselves] that God will forgive us for our misdeeds, were they not bound when they were blessed with the covenant of the written document (*mīthāq al-kitāb*), which is [the same as] the contracts (*al-ʿuhūd*) which God entered into with the sons of Israel, that they were obliged to abide by the law (*tôrah*) and act according to it? (*Jami*ʿ, vi. 143)

'Covenant' here is not concerned with worship as such but with the people of God's covenant abiding by the law and being just when executing it. In the *History*, Tabari cites a report where 'covenant' refers to an agreement between the caliph 'Uthman and the Prophet's cousin 'Ali, in which 'Uthman promises to undertake certain specified measures to meet the people's complaints against his and his governors' policies:

⟨'Ali⟩ bound ⟨'Uthman⟩ in this document as tightly as God had ever bound one of His creatures by ⟨contract (*ʿahd*)⟩ and covenant ⟨(*mīthāq*)⟩. ['Ali] had [the document] witnessed by a body of the leading Emigrants and Helpers. (*History*, xv/Humphreys. 188)

---

1 As I noted earlier (see above, p. 27, n. 1), I have preferred 'the written document' to 'the Book' when translating *kitāb*.

Here it seems that covenant (*mīthāq*) is the precondition for contract (*ʿahd*), in the form of written documents. Because of these concepts' connection to law, it can be assumed that they also refer to the social structures within which law was implemented. If we look at the Biblical covenant from this viewpoint, we find that its different forms describe a societal evolution, as it were, from tribe to state. Hence, the first covenant is between God and Noah, where God promises to sustain humans through His Creation, regardless of their sins, and Noah promises to worship God. In the second covenant between God and Abraham, God promises to provide the foundation of a state, namely a people and a territory ('the promised land'), and Abraham vows to worship none other than God, plus circumcise all male children on their eighth day, and sacrifice animals to God. However, the state still only exists as a potentiality as the territory is not yet conquered, and there is no law. Only the people, the twelve tribes of Israel, comes into being as Abraham's descendants. The law is provided in the third covenant between God and Moses, leader of the twelve tribes, when God sent down the *tôrah* on Mount Sinai, and Moses wrote it down on tablets. The law contains contractual, mutually binding obligations and rights between humans, meant to regulate their relations within the state. The fact that these are *written* is significant, for it means that they are objectively available to state functionaries, namely the scribes. However, there is still no state. Finally, in the fourth covenant between God and David, the state is founded by submitting the twelve tribes to the rule of the king under the *tôrah*, which was in the custody of the Levite priests, responsible for ensuring that it was justly implemented. Underlying all three covenants after Abraham is God's promise of 'land' as the material precondition for the state. Only God can promise land because land is part of His Creation, by which He promised to sustain the people;

thus God mirrors the head of state in the system of vassalage, who is also the only one who can assign land. Thus, the Biblical concept 'covenant' refers to the set-up of a state in the system of vassalage and its two main institutions, namely the state administration and the religious institution, with the law linked to the religious institution through its being given to the people by God's prophet, Moses.

In the Qur'an (as also in Tabari's works), the law-giver is God's Messenger, Muhammad. *Mīthāq* (lexically, bond, covenant, contract, treaty) signifies that which binds two parties in a contractual relationship with mutual obligations and rights. In Tabari's *History*, the concept is first mentioned in connection with God's creation of man, and reappears throughout in contexts of state formation or when state-related legal principles are at stake. The governing bodies referred to by *mīthāq* are the state and the religious institution. To begin with the state, Tabari's reports on Creation declare that God created man as His *khalifa* on earth. Now, *khalifa* is also the Arabic term for caliph, which directs the reader's attention to the caliphal state. According to the order of Tabari's reports, the *mīthāq* between God and man (Adam's offspring) is concluded at 'Arafat, one of the pilgrimage stations in Makka; the reference to the religious rituals brings the religious body into the picture, as in the following report from Ibn 'Abbas:

Ibn ʿAbbās [said], commenting on God's word: 'And your Lord took from the backs of the children of Adam their progeny and had them testify against themselves: Am I not your Lord? They said: Yes.' (Q. 7: 172) He rubbed Adam's back, and every living being to be created by God until the Day of Resurrection came forth at Naʿman here which is behind ʿArafat. He took their covenant {*wa akhadha mīthāqahum*}: 'Am I not your Lord? They said: Yes. We (so) testify.' (*History*, i/Rosenthal. 305)

ʿAhd is clearer than *mīthāq*, for although it is sometimes also translated as 'covenant', it refers to a 'contract' in the sense of stipulated obligations and rights. It is related to *mīthāq* in the same sense that *tôrah* is related to *berit*, namely as the 'positive law' that guides human affairs and which is possible only if the covenant is already in place. But what then *is* the covenant? It is not a written document, like the law itself, but the elevation to a universal principle of 'contractual relations', wherein the relation between God and man is paradigmatic for relations between men. The principle is mediated by the state and the religious institution in conjunction.

The notion of covenant had also more 'secular' counterparts. In *The Republic*, Plato has Socrates describe 'the social contract', which is the unwritten agreement between citizens and the state that the state and the law are the best guarantors of justice and the citizens' happiness. Another possible comparison is with Aristotle's concepts of 'constitution' (*politeia*) and 'lawgiver' (*nomothetês*), defined in *Politics*. The city state (*polis*) consists of citizens. It was founded by a lawgiver, i.e. a ruler who gave the state its law. Now, the way in which the citizens are organized, and in particular how the ruling institution functions, is regulated by a 'constitution', which is the state's 'form', or immanent organizing principle. Thus the 'constitution' is *not* written: it is not the law, but the principle that is given expression in the law. Also according to Aristotle, whether a political community is the same over time depends on whether it has the same constitution. The parallels with the covenant are that it is an unwritten principle which defines ruling institutions and thus organizes the citizens, and which was introduced by 'the lawgiver' (Prophet–Messenger) who founded the state. The idea that the constitution determines whether the political community is the same over time seems to be mirrored in the Biblical and Qur'anic accusation of violating the covenant and no longer being 'the chosen people/community'. There are of course differences too. Notably, Aristotle's constitution is immanent in the state and has nothing to do with deities, while the covenant is related to a transcendent God. However, this could be attributed to the fact that the Bible and the Qur'an were the preserve of a religious institution; hence, the covenant is a constitution that includes in its ruling institutions the religious one as custodian of the law.[1]

The constitutional and legal implications of *mīthāq* and *ʿahd* explain why Tabari gave the *History* the title *History of the Messengers and the Kings*: 'messengers' signify the religious institution and 'kings' the state. I will translate *mīthāq* as *covenant* in the sense of Aristotle's unwritten constitution which defines the governing bodies, and *ʿahd* as *contract* and *law*.

POLITICS AND METHODOLOGY

The relationship between Tabari's political objectives and his scholarly methodologies is expressed on two levels. Firstly, his scholarly preoccupation with law was political because he saw 'rule of law' as the rational form of governance, and the 'Abbasid caliphate's way out of its crisis. In *Tahdhib al-athar*, *Ikhtilaf al-fuqaha'* and the *Jami'*, he treats law in its various theoretical aspects, while in the *History* he gives concrete examples of the difference between 'rule of law' and 'arbitrariness', that is when individual and tribal interests were allowed to abuse state power and subvert the law.

Secondly, Tabari's epistemological synthesis between empiricism and idealism reflects his concern that rational governance is founded on written law, which in its turn is deduced by applying logic and analogical reasoning to

---

1 On the 'constitutional' dimensions of the Biblical covenant and the 'covenantal' aspects of Aristotle's political thought, see Elazar, *The Covenant Tradition*, especially *Vol. 3: Covenant and Constitutionalsim.*

textual, empirical sources. His insistence on using *written* records as sources is, again, an essentially political concern: the written text, whether legal or historical, is an objective source which everyone can find, study, interpret, and refer to through agreed methods. Language is then central, as the common means of communication. Tabari's rejection of allegorical interpretations comes from his refusal to depart from the empirically available surface of the text, or the explicit meaning of language, and wander into arbitrary constructions of 'hidden' meaning which anyone can concoct for the sake of a private political cause. Hence, the epistemological foundation of his methodologies reflects his fundamental but critical loyalty to the state and the body of scholarship and law associated with it. The *History* is pivotal to understanding the other works because it is there Tabari gave examples of his preferred policies, and that is the key to understanding his methodological choices.

Part 3

Tabari's *History*

CHRONOLOGICAL STRUCTURE

The following outline sets out the *History*'s chronology and contents, according to my own thematic divisions, with references to the volumes of the English translation:

Methodological Introduction. Aim; concepts; definition of time; theory of historical knowledge; sources (vol. 1, pp. 164–98).

Mythological Prelude. Development of the concepts and definitions of the methodological introduction into narratives of Creation (creation of time; living creatures; the first humans; the 'constitution'; the founding of the pilgrimage ritual; the foundation of Persian kingship; the Flood; vol. 1, pp. 198–371). The mythological prelude thus constitutes a set of assumptions about the state and society, on the basis of which the *History* is written.

Persian kings (including some Medic, Achaemenid and Arsacid kings, and all the Sassanid kings), intertwined with *Israelite* and *Arab* kings, Messengers and prophets, including the birth of the Prophet in the year 570. This is where 'real history' begins, with historical Persian kings (vols. 2–5; the

Prophet's birth is narrated in vol. 5). The kingship-model for subsequent Islamic states is Persian kingship, while the prophethood-model is that of the Israelites.

The Prophet Muhammad's mission in Makka. The Prophet's Qurayshi genealogy traced back to Abraham and Adam; the marriage to Khadija; the mission; persecution at the hands of Quraysh and invitation to Yathrib/Madina; the migration to Madina in 622; the institution of the Islamic calendar to that year (vol. 6).

The Prophet Muhammad's state in Madina. The Prophet's conquests of Makka and the Arabian Peninsula; his other marriages; instituting the rituals; his death (vols. 7–9).

The Companion Caliphates (632–61; vols. 10–17). The caliphate of Abu Bakr (632–34; vols. 10–11); of 'Umar b. al-Khattab, the conquests of the Byzantine and Sassanid empires and the expansion of the Madina state to an Islamic empire (634–44; vols. 11–14); of 'Uthman b. 'Affan (644–56; vol. 15); and 'Ali b. Abi Talib (656–61; vols. 16–17).

The Umayyad Caliphate (661–750; vols. 18–27). The Sufyanid Umayyads (vols. 18–20); the Marwanid Umayyads (vols. 20–7).

The 'Abbasid Caliphate (750–915; vols. 27–38). The 'Abbasid revolution against the Umayyads and founding of their dynasty (vol. 27); the foundation of Baghdad and the 'Abbasid 'golden age' (vols. 28–30); civil war among 'Abbasid factions (vol. 31); brief reunification of the 'Abbasid caliphate (vol. 32); the long decline (vols. 33–38).

Tabari was born in the year 838, which is chronicled in volume 33. Thus his life coincided with the turn of 'Abbasid political power from success to decline. The period 870–908, which saw a brief revival of state power, is more or less covered by volumes 37 and 38.

BIBLICAL STRUCTURE

A second set of structures is related to the terms 'messengers' and 'kings', which in turn are connected to the Bible. In the Introduction to the *History*, Tabari stated his aim:

In this book of mine, I shall mention whatever information has reached us about kings throughout the ages from when our Lord began the creation of His creation to its annihilation. There were messengers sent by God, kings placed in authority, or caliphs established in the caliphal succession. (*History*, i/Rosenthal. 168)

Elsewhere, Tabari also used the term 'prophet'. So he in fact had four categories: Messengers and prophets, and kings and caliphs (the list below sets out the ones he treated). A hybrid category, 'the prophet-kings' (David, Solomon and Muhammad), were heads of state and prophets at the same time – they received revelations *and* founded the sanctuaries for the worship of God. The Companion caliphs are caliphs because elected through consultation and on merit; they represent a period when succession was based on the principle of merit. The Umayyad and 'Abbasid caliphates are caliphates only in name; having instituted dynastic succession in place of meritocracy, they are in effect 'kingship' (see above, p. 21):

Messengers: Noah; Lot; Isma'il; Moses; Jesus; Hud; Salih; Shu'ayb; Muhammad (610–32)
Prophets: Noah; Lot; Abraham; Isma'il; Isaac; Jacob; Joseph; Moses; Aaron; David; Solomon; Idris; Job; Jonah; Elijah; Elisha; Zechariah; John the Baptist; Jesus; Muhammad (610–32)
Prophet-kings: David; Solomon; Muhammad 622–32
Caliphate ('meritocracy'): Abu Bakr (632–34); 'Umar (634–44); 'Uthman (644–56); 'Ali (656–61)
Kingship: Israelite kingship to 586 BC; Iranian kingship to 640; Arab kingship (Syria: Ghassan; Mesopotamia: Lakhm; Yemen: Himyar); Umayyads 661–750; 'Abbasids 750–915

Most of the Messengers and prophets, and two of the prophet-kings, are Biblical characters. Of course, a bare list of their names does not reflect the way they are actually presented in the *History*. However, the thematic similarities show up clearly when we set the Hebrew Bible's chronological outline side by side with that of the *History*:

Figure 1

The Hebrew Bible	The *History*
Genesis: Creation and ancestry (the patriarchs' covenant)	Pre-Islamic history: Creation and ancestry of Messengers and kings (the covenant of creation, the patriarchs' covenant and the kings of Israel, Persia, and the Arabs)
Exodus—Deut.: Moses' Sinai covenant, revelation, foundation of community	The Prophet's covenant, revelation, foundation of community and the city-state
Joshua: Conquest of the promised land of Canaan and the founding of the state	The caliphate of 'Umar: Conquest of the promised land (the Sawad) and founding of the imperial state
Judges: Just rule in the promised land	Remainder of the Companion caliphs: Just rule in the promised land
Kings, *Chronicles*, *Prophets*: Royal justice and oppression; prophetic guidance of kings	The Umayyad caliphate: Caliphal justice and oppression; *Ahl al-bayt* and Companion guidance
Ezra and *Nehemiah*: Restoration of Moses' covenant in the promised land of Canaan under universal Persian kingship	The 'Abbasid caliphate: Restoration of the Prophet's covenant in the promised land (the Sawad) under Islamic universal kingship

The reason for thematic correspondences between the Hebrew Bible and the *History* may be their common reference to 'covenant' as underlying relations between the state and religious institutions, both within the system of vassalage.

The question arises: how did Biblical material get into the *History*? There were, among the early historians, several Jewish and Christian converts. These 'convert historians' appear as authorities in *isnad*s to some of Tabari's reports containing Biblical material. In the Companion generation, there is 'Abd Allah b. Salam, rabbi from Madina, and Ka'b al-Ahbar, rabbi of Yemeni origin. Among the next generation, that of the Successors, we find Wahb b. Munabbih, a

Jew of Yemeni, Persian origins, and Muhammad b. Ishaq, whose grandfather was a Christian (probably Nestorian) from Iraq. In their reports, material from the Bible, the Mishna, the Talmud, the Targums, and the Haggadic literature, appears in the form of explicit citations and implicit themes.

The reports of Muhammad b. Ishaq (d. 767) occupy a central place in Tabari's *History*. Ibn Ishaq wrote the standard biography of the Prophet, shaping it so as to present him as the Saviour prophesied in the Biblical books of Isaiah and Jeremiah. He collected reports from his native town Madina, and later also from Alexandria, Kufa, and Rayy, after which he settled in Baghdad. There he was employed by the second 'Abbasid caliph al-Mansur to educate the successor al-Mahdi in the Prophet's biography and early history of the caliphate – a trajectory not dissimilar to Tabari's. Ibn Ishaq sometimes derived Biblical or Jewish-Christian information directly from 'some scholar(s) from the people of the first Book [i.e. the Hebrew Bible]'. (For a good example, see the citation of *Genesis* 4. 9–16, translated into Arabic from Biblical Aramaic, in *History*, i/Rosenthal. 312.)

The totality of Ibn Ishaq's reports cover four historical subjects, namely 'The Beginning' (or 'Genesis,' (*al-mubtada'*); 'The Mission' (*al-mab'ath*); 'The Campaigns' (*al-maghāzī*); and 'The Caliphs' (or 'The Successors', *al-khulafā'*). He sometimes also cited reports transmitted by earlier convert historians, for example Wahb b. Munabbih, who transmitted Yemeni Jewish and Christian traditions. Ibn Ishaq's reports now exist only in two forms: in the abridged edition of his work by the historian Ibn Hisham (d. 833), containing 'The Mission' and 'The Campaigns,' i.e. without either the 'Biblical' mythology or the caliphal history; and in Tabari's *History*, where material from all four subject areas is cited and constitutes a backbone for Tabari's sections on the

Israelite prophets and the Prophet's biography. Tabari learned two different recensions of Ibn Ishaq's material. Mostly he used the one he received in al-Rayy from Ibn Humayd (d. 862), who transmitted it from the *qadi* Salama b. al-Fadl (d. 806). The other was from the Kufan Abu Kurayb (d. 861), from Yunus b. Bukayr (d. 814) – this is the one edited by Ibn Hisham. The net effect of Ibn Ishaq's prophetic history, as transmitted by Tabari, is to make the Prophet the embodiment of all previous Messengers. (It is probably significant that Ibn Ishaq was of Christian origins, as just this technique had been used in the New Testament to present Jesus as the fulfilment of the Hebrew Bible's prophecies about a future Saviour.)

Another important authority is the Prophet's cousin and Companion 'Abdallah b. 'Abbas (d. 687), who appears frequently in the *History* and the *Jami'*. Although not a convert from Judaism or Christianity, his speciality was, like Ibn Ishaq, to recast Biblical material according to the principle that the Prophet and Islam are the fulfilment of Biblical prophesies. He plays the part also of the Inquisitor in relation to the convert historians, alert lest they distort Islamic teachings by introducing ideas from their former religions (*History*, i/Rosenthal. 232–3).

In Tabari's reports from Ibn Ishaq, the Prophet is presented, by the transfer to him of literary motifs from Biblical characters, as the embodiment of all previous Messengers, prophets and prophet-kings. Abraham is the first such model. In the Bible, he comes from Mesopotamia and wanders to Canaan on God's commands. Abraham's covenant is the first, in which God promises him a people and the land of Canaan. In the *History*, God's important transactions with Abraham are moved from Mesopotamia and Canaan to Makka and the Ka'ba, Islam's central sanctuary:

Hishām b. Muḥammad—his father: {…} The Kaʿbah had been destroyed when the people of Noah were drowned, and God

commanded his friend Abraham and Abraham's son Ismael to rebuild it on its original foundations. This they did, as is stated in the Qurʾān. And when Abraham and Ismael were raising the foundations of the House (Abraham prayed): 'Our Lord! Accept from us [this duty]. Only You are the Hearer, the Knower.'
{The Kaʿba} had not had any custodians since its destruction in the time of Noah. Then God commanded Abraham to settle his son by the Kaʿbah, wishing thereby to show a mark of esteem to one whom he later ennobled by means of his Prophet Muḥammad. Abraham, the Friend of the Compassionate, and his son Ismael were custodians of the Kaʿbah after the time of Noah. At that time, Mecca was uninhabited, and the surrounding country was inhabited by the Jurhum and ʿAmāliqah. (*History*, vi/Watt & McDonald. 51–2)

The chart below illustrates the transfer of motifs: a motif related to Abraham in the Bible is found also in Tabari's reports about Abraham in the *History*, and also in Tabari's reports about the Prophet:

Figure 2

Abraham in the Hebrew Bible	Abraham in the *History*	The Prophet in the *History*
Ancestor of the chosen people, promised the land (*Gen.* 12. 1–3)	Ancestor of monotheistic priestly lineage, Āl ʿImrān (ii. 62, 67–8)	Ancestor of family within monotheistic priestly lineage through Abraham, Quraysh (vi. 1–3)
Visits Jerusalem, later central sanctuary in promised land. Priestly king distributes wine and bread (*Gen.* 14. 18)	Visits Makka, later central sanctuary in holy land. Erects the Kaʿba on Adam's foundation (ii. 69–71)	Rebuilds the Kaʿba in the holy land on Abraham's foundation (vi. 51–3)
Nearly sacrifices Isaac (*Gen.* 22)	Nearly sacrifices Isaac (ii. 83–5)	His grandfather nearly sacrificed his son ʿAbdallah (vi. 1–3)

The next important Messenger and prophet is Moses, 'the lawgiver'. The parallels between Moses and the Prophet are more numerous than with any other prophet or Messenger:

Figure 3

Moses in the *History* <Moses in the Hebrew Bible>	The Prophet in the *History*
Of priestly Levite lineage (v. 30) <*Exodus* 2. 1–2>	Of priestly Qurayshi/ Hashimi lineage (vi. 16–18)
Almost orphan (iii. 34–5) <Orphan; *Exodus* 2. 3–6>	Orphan (vi. 44–5)
Almost suckled by wet nurse (iii. 35) <Suckled by wet nurse; *Exodus* 2. 7–9>	Suckled by wet nurse (v. 272–4)
Pursued by Pharaoh (iii. 33–5) <*Exodus* 2, 14>	Pursued by Jews, Byzantines, and Quraysh (vi. 45–6, 93–5)
Shepherd (iii. 49–51) <*Exodus* 3. 1>	Shepherd (vi. 47; v. 282)
Addressed by bush (iii. 50–1) <*Exodus* 3:4>	Addressed by trees and stones (vi. 63–4)
Receives the law in desert on Mount Sinai (iii. 76–8) <*Exodus* 19–21>	Receives the law in desert on Mount Hira' (vi. 67–9)
Ascends to God (iii. 76–8) <*Exodus* 19:20>	Ascends to God (vi. 78–81)
Redistributes meat, cereal, water, God's law (iii. 76–8) <*Exodus*>	Redistributes meat, cereal, milk, God's law (vi. 78–81, 90)
Emigrates (iii. 76–8) <*Exodus*>	Emigrates (al-Hijra) (vi. 145–7)
Founds community governed by the law (iii. 78–80) <*Exodus*>	Founds community governed by the law (viii)
Combats idol worship (iii. 73–5) <*Exodus* 32>	Combats idol worship (vi. 46–7, 88–9; viii. 187–8)
Brother Aaron helper in ritual and against Pharaoh (iii. 52–4) <*Exodus* 4. 14–16, 27–31>	Cousin 'Ali helper in ritual and against Quraysh (vi. 80–2, 142–4; ix. 51, 110–11)

Raids against inhabitants of the promised land (iii. 94) <*Num.* 21:1–3, 21–35; 31>	Raids against inhabitants of the holy land (vii. 26–69)
Buried outside the promised land (iii. 85–87) <*Deut.* 34. 5–6>	Buried outside the promised land (ix. 163–209)
Successor Joshua conquers the promised land (iii. 85–98) <*Joshua*>	Successor 'Umar conquers the promised land (xii. 84, 122–61)

The next great figure is David, the first 'prophet-king'. In the Bible, David's covenant introduces kingship as ruling institution. Moreover, from the post-exilic perspective, his kingship signifies the hope for a restored future kingship in the Promised Land. However, while all the parallels between Moses and the Prophet are found on all three textual levels (the Bible, Moses in the *History*, and the Prophet in the *History*), all the parallels to David are not. In some cases, there is a correspondence across all three levels but in other cases correspondences between the Biblical David and the Prophet in the *History* are not found for David in the *History*:

Figure 4

David in the *History* <David in the Hebrew Bible>	The Prophet in the *History*
Shepherd (iii. 136) <*1 Sam.* 17. 15>	Shepherd (v. 282; vi. 47)
Saul tries to kill fake image of David (iii. 137) <*1 Sam.* 19:11–17>	Quraysh try to kill 'Ali made out to be the Prophet (vi. 142–3)
Pursued by Saul (iii. 137–138) <*1 Sam.* 21>	Pursued by Quraysh (vi. 139–44)
Hid from Saul in cave (iii. 137) <*1 Sam.* 22. 1>	Hid from Quraysh in cave (vi. 146)
<King over tribal group of Judah in Hebron; *2 Sam.* 2. 3–4>	Leader over Muslims in Makka (vi. 80–144)
<War between tribal groups of Israel and Judah; *2 Sam.* 2. 12–3. 1>	War between tribal groups of Aws and Khazraj (vi. 123)
<Invited to become king by tribal	Invited to become head of

group of Israel; *2 Sam.* 5. 1–2>	state by tribal coalition al-Ansar (vi. 124–6)
King over Israel and Judah in Hebron; *2 Sam.* 5. 3–4>	Head of state over al-Muhajirun and al-Ansar in Madina (viii)
<Conquers central sanctuary through the allied forces of Israel and Judah; *2 Sam.* 5. 6–7>	Conquers central sanctuary through the allied forces of al-Muhajirun and al-Ansar (viii. 160–2)

Lastly, there is Jesus, descendant of King David on his father's side and of the priestly Aaronites on his mother's side. In the New Testament, he represents a new covenant, portrayed as the fulfilment of the Hebrew Bible's prophecies of a restored kingdom, albeit one divested from the land of Canaan. As with David, we again find some instances of correspondences across the three textual levels, and also instances where correspondences are lacking from Jesus narratives in the *History*:

Figure 5

Jesus in the *History* <Jesus in the New Testament>	The Prophet in the *History*
Born under a rising star (iv. 116, 125) <*Matt.* 2. 2>	Born under a rising star (v. 271)
Tempted by the devil (iv. 118) <*Luke* 4. 1–13; *Matt.* 4. 1–11; *Mark* 1. 12–13>	Tempted by the devil (vi. 107–9)
Romans and Jews plot to kill him (iv. 114, 116, 125) <*passim*>	Romans, Jews, and Quraysh plot to kill him (vi. 45–6, 93–5)
Ascends to God (iv. 122, 125) <*Matt.* 28; *Mark* 16; *Luke* 24; *John* 20>	Ascends to God (vi. 78–80)
Sends out apostles (iv. 122–4) <*Acts*>	Sends out messengers (viii. 98–100)
<Mary's annunciation; *Luke* 1. 31–3>	Amina's annunciation (v. 269)
<Simeon attests his status as Saviour; (*Luke* 2. 22–35>	Waraqa attests his status as Saviour (vi. 72)
<Message rejected in hometown;	Message rejected in

Luke 4. 16–30>	hometown (vi. 88–115)
<Reinterprets Moses' law ('Sermon on the mount'); *Matt.* 5–7>	Reinterprets Moses' law (vi. 72)
<Redistribution of cereal, fish, and wine ('feeding miracle', 'last supper'); *Matt.* 14. 13–21, 26. 26–9>	Redistribution of cereal, meat, and milk (vi. 90)

The most detailed and complete set of correspondences is between Moses and the Prophet. For David and Jesus, the narrative elements that we find in the Bible associated with their roles as ideal king and saviour have been omitted from the narratives about them in Tabari's *History* and transferred straight to the Prophet, who is thus the prophesied saviour–king, but in the style of Moses as 'the law-giver'.

METHODOLOGICAL INTRODUCTION

Tabari's methodological Introduction presents the issues dealt with in the *History* in terms of models and definitions. Both in its original and in the English translation, this Introduction is a very beautiful exposé. My account here cannot do justice to the full version; I can only illustrate the relationship between Tabari's concept of God and his methodological considerations. We will begin by outlining the contents of the Introduction, followed by a more detailed exploration:

Invocation of God and *definition of the concept of God* (i. 165).

Description of God's blessings and *human responses* (i. 166–8).

Aim of the History, i.e. to write history in terms of how 'messengers, kings and caliphs' responded to God's blessings (i. 168–9).

Short definition of time (i. 169).

Sources, source-critical method, and *theory of historical knowledge* (i. 170–1).

The opening *invocation of God* defines God's nature:

Praised be God, first before any first and last after any last, enduring without cease and persevering in everything without moving away, Creator of His creation from no original or model. He is singular and unique without number. He remains after everyone infinitely without term. His are glory and greatness, splendour and might, authority and power. He is above having a partner in His authority, or in His uniqueness having one like Him, or in His administration an aid or helper, or having a child or spouse or 'any equal' {Q. 112. 4}. He cannot be fully imagined and encompassed by the regions {Q. 55. 33} and 'reached by the eyes while He reaches them. He is subtle and knowledgeable. {Q. 6. 103}' (*History*, i/Rosenthal. 165)

This whole passage, with its emphasis on God's non-comparability to created beings, defines a concept of God which is consciously distancing itself from the Trinity and its 'humanized' concept of God (or deified humanity). The invocation continues with Tabari expressing his gratitude to God, and supplicating His aid in doing what pleases Him:

I praise Him for His benefits and am grateful to Him for His favours in the manner befitting one who singles Him out for praise and who hopes to receive more (favors) from Him for having been grateful. I ask Him to grant me to say and do what will bring me close to Him and please Him. I believe in Him as one who declares oneness belonging exclusively to Him and who reserves glorification for Him alone. (Ibid)

Reserving glorification for God alone is an intrinsic part of the concept of God as different from His creatures: all humans are equal before God the Creator – and therefore no human is faultless in the eyes of Tabari the historian.

In the next section on *God's blessings and human responses* (ibid, 166), we have the first example of the covenant and its contractual obligations: God is obliged to sustain humans through the material resources contained in His creation, while humans are obliged to worship God. Material creation is the first blessing. The second is reason, which enables man to distinguish between true and false, useful and harmful, and make rational use of the material resources by which God has blessed him:

> In this fleeting and manifold world, His many manifestations of generosity and bounty include and encompass all human beings. He gave them ears, eyes, and hearts and singled them out for possessing reason which makes it possible for them to distinguish between truth and falsehood and to recognize what is useful and what is harmful. He made the earth for them a carpet, so that they would have there passable roads to walk on, {Q. 71. 19–20} and 'the heaven a well-guarded roof' {Q. 21. 32} and a lofty construction. From it He brought down for them plentiful rain and sizable sustenance. (Ibid, 166)

After this Tabari describes how God created the sun and moon, so that humans would be able to distinguish day from night and define the times for the acts of worship God has commanded them to do, namely prayer, charity, pilgrimage and fasting, as well as the times for 'settling their debts and their claims', including taxes; thus the preconditions for fulfilling contractual obligations are here described as being part of God's creation, namely the planets after which time is measured.

Humans respond to God's blessings in two principal ways, by being grateful or ungrateful. Human gratitude is reciprocated by God increasing His favours in this life and combining that with bliss in the hereafter. As for the ungrateful who deny God's favours and worship some other, His favours may be withdrawn from them in this life and replaced by punishment, or they may be respited so that their load in the hereafter is heavier, their punishment then more deserved (ibid, 167–8). Reciprocity is implied in the covenantal contract: God responds to human responses to His blessings, which is to say that He does not act arbitrarily but according to the terms of a mutually obligating, contractual relationship.

Against this background, Tabari proceeds to state the aim of his *History*, which was to study blessings and responses specifically in relation to the 'messengers and kings', limiting himself to the main events during their reigns, their death, and the succession:

In this book of mine, I shall mention whatever information has reached us about kings throughout the ages from when our Lord began the creation of His Creation to its annihilation. There were messengers sent by God, kings placed in authority, or caliphs established in the caliphal succession. God had early on bestowed His benefits and favors upon them. Some were grateful for His favors and He thus gave them more favors and bounty in addition to those bestowed by Him upon them in their fleeting life, or He postponed the increase and stored it up for them with Himself. There were others who were not grateful for His favors, and so He deprived them of the favors He had bestowed upon them early on and hastened for them His revenge. There were also others who were not grateful for His favors; He let them enjoy them until the time of their death and perdition. Every one of them whom I shall mention in this book of mine will be mentioned in conjunction with his time but (only) summaries of the events in his day and age will be added, since an exhaustive treatment is not possible in a lifetime and makes books too long. This will be combined with references to the length of their natural life and the time of their death. (Ibid, 168)

The next issue in Tabari's Introduction is time (ibid, 169). He asks what it is, its total extent, its beginning and end, whether anything was before God created time, what will be after its annihilation, if anything remains 'other than the face (*wajh*) of the Highly praised, the Exalted Creator?' According to Tabari, only God is eternal and non-contingent, while all time is finite and created by Him. Tabari also states that, for the purpose of the History, philosophical discussions of time are not relevant. What matters is how to measure historical time:

the dates of past kings {...} and summaries of their history, the times of the messengers and prophets and how long they lived, the days of the early caliphs and some of their biographical data, and the extent of the territories under their control, as well as the events that took place in their age. (Ibid, 169)

Tabari's concern about the dynamics between rational government and imperial might may be hinted in 'the extent of the territories under the [early caliphs'] control'.

Next, Tabari explains that he has weighed the merits of the reporters transmitting information about the remote and near past, and why he has done so:

I do this for the purpose of clarifying whose transmission {of traditions} is praised and whose information is accepted, whose transmission is rejected and whose is disregarded, and whose tradition is considered feeble and whose information is considered weak. In addition, I give the reason why someone's information is disregarded and the cause for someone's tradition being considered feeble. (Ibid, 170)

This is no different from the source-critical evaluations that every historian has to do. The information which Tabari used for his source-critique is appended to the *History* as *Dhayl al-mudhayyal* (lit. 'The Supplemented Supplement', vol. 39 in the English translation), which is a biographical section containing information about the first generations of scholars.

Tabari's method is founded on a theory of historical knowledge, a distinction between knowledge about a past event or time which is gained from eye-witnesses or people living in the same time, and knowledge which is based on the historian's reasoning and logic and so pertains to the historian, not to the people of the past time. Reasoning cannot be a source of historical knowledge. It is, however, the source of historical analysis: on the basis of primary source-based historical information, the historian can, through deductive reasoning, analyse the causes of historical development:

The reader should know that with respect to all I have mentioned and made it a condition to set down in this writing of ours, I rely upon traditions and reports which I have transmitted and which I attribute to their transmitters. I rely only very exceptionally upon what is learned through rational arguments and deduced by thought processes. For no knowledge of the history of men of the past and of recent men and events is attainable by those who were not able to observe them and did not live in their time, except through information and transmission provided by informants and transmitters. This cannot be brought out by reason or deduced by thought processes. This writing of mine may [be found to] contain some information, mentioned by us on the authority of certain men of the past, which the reader may disapprove of and the listener may find detestable, because he can find nothing sound and no real meaning in it. In such cases, he should know that such information has come to him not from us, but from those who transmitted it to us. We have merely reported it as it was reported to us. (Ibid, 170–1)

Thus, the methodological Introduction informs the reader that Tabari intended to study the extent to which different Messengers, kings and caliphs were 'grateful' to God, that is, employed reason in governing their peoples and using their material resources. Tabari also states that he uses only primary sources for the empirical historical information, while using deductive reasoning to evaluate whether or not their government was rational, which he does within the parameters of the system of vassalage.

MYTHOLOGICAL PRELUDE

Tabari's methodological Introduction lays out the basic concepts and analytical framework of the *History*. It is followed by a mythological prelude to history proper. 'Mythological' here refers to narratives about the creation of the material world and the founding of society's most basic institutions. In the *History*, these are: time measures, the planets, vegetation and all living organisms including man, the first covenant, and the governing bodies pertaining to Persian kingship.

The fact that Tabari began the *History* with narratives of the creation has led scholars to suggest that he held the driving force of history to be God's will, effectuated through the choices of powerful individuals:

That the economy or climate worked independently of, much less counter to, God's will, was virtually unthinkable: historians [like and including Tabari] understood the world to be an integrated and ordered whole, all its occupants being subject to God's sovereignty. Just rulers enjoyed God's favour and witnessed peace and prosperity. But when the fish rotted, it rotted from the head down: an unjust governor appointed rapacious tax collectors, who, in over-taxing, might rob the farmers of the seed corn they needed for the following year, which would mean famine. The whole system fell out of balance.[1]

However, if, as I have argued, Tabari wrote history to explore the effects of rational and irrational government, the question of whether governors enacted God's will is irrelevant: their choices had consequences, and it is these consequences which were Tabari's concern. And yet it is also true, as Robinson pointed out, that Tabari conceived of human choices as enacted within certain parameters. But in order to understand what Tabari thought these parameters were, and God's role in setting them, we need to look closely at his narratives about the creation of time.

As we have seen, Tabari stated that only God is eternal and that He created time. However, time was not the first thing God created, for the first thing God created was the Pen:

Ibn ʿAbbās {…} used to tell that the Messenger of God said: 'The first thing created by God is the Pen. God commanded it to write everything (*wa-amarahu an yaktuba kulla shayʾ*).' (*History*, i/ Rosenthal. 199)

---

[1] Robinson, *Islamic Historiography*, 130.

This Prophetic tradition could be understood as meaning that everything that is written is predetermined. However, this is not necessarily the case. The relevant matter is in two reports on the subject of the Pen, with the issue being how one translates and understands the concept *qadar*. In Franz Rosenthal's translation, I have underlined the relevant phrases, followed by an alternative rendering:

According to Wāṣil b. ʿAbd al-Aʿlā al-Asadī – Muḥammad b. Fuḍayl – al-Aʿmash – Abū Ẓabyān – Ibn ʿAbbās: The first thing created by God is the Pen. God said to it: 'Write!', whereupon the Pen asked: 'What shall I write, my Lord?' God replied: 'Write what is predestined {*uktub al-qadar*}!' He continued. And the Pen proceeded to (write) whatever is predestined and going to be to the Coming of the Hour {*fajara al-qalam bimā huwa kāʾin min dhālika ilā qiyām al-sāʿa*}. Then, (God) lifted up the water vapor and split the heavens off from it. (Ibid, 200)

[*alternative rendering*: …] 'What shall I write, my Lord?' God replied: 'Write the measured capacities [*uktub al-qadar*]!' He continued: And the Pen proceeded to (write) what can be to the Coming of the Hour (*fajara al-qalam bimā huwa kāʾin min dhālika ilā qiyām al-sāʿa*). […]

From Ibn Bashshār – ʿAbd al-Raḥmān – Sufyān – Abū Hāshim – Mujāhid: I said to Ibn ʿAbbās: There are people who consider predestination {*al-qadar*} untrue? He said: (Then), they consider the Book of God untrue! I shall seize one of them by the hair and shake him up. God was on His Throne before He created anything. The first (thing) created by God was the Pen. It proceeded to (write) whatever is going to be to the Day of Resurrection {*fajara bimā huwa kāʾin ilā yawm al-qiyāma*}. People will proceed merely in accordance with what is a foregone conclusion (decided by predestination and written down by the Pen) {*wa innamā yajri al-nās ʿalā amrin qad furigha minhu*}. (Ibid, 201–2)

[*alternative rendering*: …] I said to Ibn 'Abbas: There are people who consider the [measured] capacity (*al-qadar*) to be untrue? […] [The Pen] proceeded to write what can be until the Day of Resurrection (*fajara bimā huwa kāʾin ilā yawm al-qiyāma*). Thus people proceed according to what has been settled [in terms of capacity] (*wa innamā yajri al-nās ʿalā amrin qad furigha minhu*).

The Arabic *qadar* refers specifically to 'that which God has meted out', and as such is equivalent to the term *qadr*, 'measure': that which God has meted out (*qadar*) is a certain measure (*qadr*) of sustenance, years, intellect, health, wealth, etc.[1] *Qadar* can also mean 'the sum of something' (*mablagh al-shayʾ*), i.e. the totality of what has been meted out.[2] In reference to God, it has a clear connotation of power, in the sense that God has the capacity to mete out the measures and effectuate all that He wills. In reference to humans, *qadar* refers to what God has meted out to each, the sum total of what an individual has at his or her disposal, the individual's capacities. Thus it is legitimate to render the sentence *uktub al-qadar* as 'Write the measured capacities!' It should also be noted that the implications of the term *qadar* were contested in medieval Islamic theology as well. The Jabriyya ('the school of divine enforcement') understood it in the sense that God has meted out for each individual a capacity which compels action according to only one (predetermined) course. However, the Qadariyya ('the school of capacity') took *qadar* as a personal capacity to choose between several possible courses of action.

In the context of Tabari's history writing, assuming the suggested translation of *qadar* is correct, it is not right to say that he perceived history as the effectuation of God's will, except in the trivial sense that nothing can ever have happened that God has not enabled. Tabari stated in the Introduction that God perceives some human actors as 'grateful' and others as 'ungrateful', and He rewards and punishes them accordingly; thus God has not predetermined their choices, only the range of possibilities within which

1 *Lisān al-ʿarab*, under *qadar*.

2 *Tāj al-ʿarūs*, under *qadar*.

their choices are effectuated. This is in line with a legal theory of contract, namely that the parties have the choice of honouring or violating a contract, though, rationally, they should honour their obligations. Moreover, it makes little sense for any historian to merely trace a predetermined development – especially not in the case of Tabari, who wanted his works to inspire new practices.

Outside the context of Tabari's *History*, in his theological works, the central question is not *which* choices were made but about whether there is such a thing as human free will, or divine measuring. Tabari would give stronger emphasis to the latter. This seems to be the case in *Tahdhib al-athar*, where Tabari discusses a Prophetic tradition reported by 'Ali b. Abi Talib:

> ʿAlī [...] said: 'The Messenger of God said: "Neither jaundice nor venom will pass from a sickly person to a healthy person." ' I [Thaʿlaba] said: 'Did you really hear this from the Prophet?' [ʿAlī] said: 'Yes.' (*Tahdhib*, iv. 3: 'Musnad ʿAlī b. Abī Ṭālib')

Tabari holds this to be a sound, truthful tradition, in spite of its surprising contents (that a healthy person cannot catch a disease from a sick one). He explains the tradition against the background of the practices of the People of Ignorance (*ahl al-jāhiliyya*), such as augury, and avoiding the sick out of fear of contracting their disease through food or drink or proximity, or other forms of contact. The excessive anxiety prompting such practices is futile; the Prophet taught his community that everything – good and bad – that happened to any of God's creatures was already contained in the writing. (Ibid, 16)

In the *History*, Tabari's concept of measuring of human capacities is related to two concepts of time which he deploys in his section on God's creation, *al-duhūr* and *al-azmān*. *Duhūr* (sing. *dahr*) refers to 'creation' as a measured time span, while *azmān* (sing. *zaman*) is 'time' in the mundane sense of hours, days, weeks, and so on. Only God is eternal and non-contingent. Creation is not eternal, because God created it and therefore it has a beginning and an end; it is a *qadar*, 'measure'. Creation came into being when God had created the first thing, the Pen. As we saw in the reports cited above, God commanded the Pen to write every thing and all that can be until the final Hour. The Pen thus wrote a scene with innumerable possibilities and individuals, and this scene is creation. The Pen is part of creation, not of God, and therefore one cannot say that *what* the Pen wrote is an expression of God's will: God merely commanded the Pen *to* write, and the rest is history.

According to Tabari, mundane time (*azmān*) was created after the Pen and its writing down of *al-qadar*, when God created the sun and the moon (*History*, i/Rosenthal. 198–202, 228–49). God 'knows' all of creation because the time measures that give humans the impression that time moves 'forward' do not apply to God, Who exists outside of them in eternity: He views the whole scene from an eternal, motionless above. Humans, living in worldly time, do not know *al-qadar* and have no overview of the whole range of possibilities open to them, or of the consequences of their choices. Therefore they must use reason to make the most rational choices. Historical writing may assist them in this purpose, by providing examples of past choices.

The concept of creation as a measure means that it has a definite end in time, when every individual will answer to God for his or her choices. Tabari devoted a long section to 'the total measure of time from its beginning to its end' (ibid, 172–86), including a reflection on the consternating circumstance that each religious community has its own measure of the total extent of time is, depending on its particular creation myths and scriptures. For example, the time from the creation of Adam to the Hijra (the Prophet's migration from Makka to Madina, 622) is, according to the Jews, 4642 years; according to the Greek Christians, 5992 years; according to the Magians (Zoroastrians) assuming their Jayumart as 'father of mankind' is Adam, 3139 years (ibid, 184–5). Tabari concludes, after his deliberations, that the total amount of time is seven thousand years, as reported by Ibn 'Abbas from the Prophet (ibid, 183) This gave rise to a new question: How much time was left? Tabari calculates that 6500 years had passed by the Hijra, leaving (out of the remaining five hundred before the Hour of Reckoning) some two hundred years or so after Tabari's own days.

Tabari's calculations about the whole of time aside, his question about the duration of time was motivated by the practical difficulty for the historian of locating events in time before the Islamic calendar, because there was no universally agreed upon time measure before that. After the Hijra, the *History* is structured as a chronicle, year by year. For events before the Hijra, Tabari's solution was to go by the Persian king lists and weave accounts about the Israelite and Arab Messengers and kings around them, because Persian history was the best chronicled:

> The history (or chronology) of the world's bygone years is more easily explained and more clearly seen based upon the lives of the Persian kings than upon those of the kings of any other nation. For no nation but theirs among those leading their pedigree back to Adam is known whose realm lasted and whose rule was continuous. No other nation had kings ruling all (their subjects) and chiefs protecting them against their adversaries, helping them to obtain the upper hand over their competitors, defending those wronged among them against those who did them wrong and creating for them fortunate conditions that were continuous, lasting, and orderly, inherited by later generations from the earlier ones. Thus, a history based upon the lives of the Persian kings has the soundest sources and the best and clearest data. (Ibid, 319; see also *History*, ii/Brinner. 133–4)

Evidently, Tabari saw Persian kingship as providing both chronology and models for imperial government. There is also a connection between the mythical origins of Persian kingship lore and his native Tabaristan. According to a myth he reports, Jayumart (the 'first man' and Persian equivalent of Adam) was 'a long-lived lord who settled on the mountain of Dunbawand of the Tabaristan mountains in the East and ruled there and in Fars. His power grew and, he commanded his children to take control of Babil [Babylon]' (*History*, i/Rosenthal. 318).

In Tabari's narrative of Adam and Eve in the Garden, and their temptation and banishment, the events take place around Makka and the Ka'ba sanctuary. Below is cited a report about Adam founding the Ka'ba or 'the House' (*al-bayt*). In the Garden, Adam had been enjoying the presence of God and the angels, and he missed their company after he was cast down to earth, landing in India. Being of enormous stature, he used to stick his head through the heavens up into the Garden and call to them. The angels complained about this to God, Who reduced Adam's height so that he lost touch with them. Adam complained to God:

According to {...} Ibn ʿAbbās: When Adam's size was lowered to sixty cubits, he started to say: My {L}ord! I was Your protégé in Your house, having no Lord but You and no one to watch out for me except You. There I had plenty to eat and could dwell wherever I wanted. But then you cast me down to this holy mountain. (There,) I used to hear the voices of the angels and see them crowd around Your Throne and to enjoy the sweet smell of Paradise. Then You cast me down to earth and reduced me to sixty cubits. I was cut off from the voices and the sight (of the angels) and the smell of Paradise left me. God replied: Because of your disobedience have I done this to you, Adam. {...} Then God revealed to Adam: I have a sacred territory around My Throne. Go and build a house for Me there! Then crowd around it, as you have seen My angels crowd around My Throne. There I shall respond to you and all your children who are obedient to Me. Adam said: My Lord! How could I do that? I do not have the strength to do it and do not know how. So God chose an angel to assist him, and he went with him toward Mecca. {...} He built the House with (materials from) five mountains: Mount Sinai, the Mount of Olives, (Mount) Lebanon, and al-Jūdī, and he constructed its foundations with (materials from Mount) Ḥirāʾ

(near Mecca). When he finished with its construction, the angel went out with him to ʿArafāt. He showed him all the rites (connected with the pilgrimage) that people perform today. Then he went with him to Mecca, and (Adam) circumambulated the House for a week. Returning to India, he died upon (Mount) Nūdh. (Ibid, 293–5)

The Kaʿba was built on the spot where God had thrown down a jewel from the Garden, which indicates that it was located right beneath His Throne in the Garden. The report also describes the central rite of the annual pilgrimage (*ḥajj*), when the pilgrims in their white garments circle the Kaʿba in imitation of the angels' crowding around God's Throne in the Garden. The rite thus signifies that the pilgrim comes to stand before God's Throne, face to face with Him. As such, it is the ritual gestation of the covenant as precondition for the legal contract and its mutually obligating conditions.

This connection between the pilgrimage and the covenant is reinforced by another report (cited above, p. 51) describing how God took the mythical covenant pledge from mankind on the plain of ʿArafat, one of the pilgrimage stations around Makka. In response to God's call 'Am I not your Lord?', each individual affirms the contractual obligations: 'Yes, we so testify'. That the Kaʿba was held to have a special significance as *locus* for the mythical covenant is perhaps expressed in a report about an exchange between the caliph Muʿawiya (r. 661–80) and Ibn al-Zubayr, which took place by the Kaʿba. Muʿawiya asked Ibn al-Zubayr if he would stick to his promise to swear allegiance to him, and the latter replied: 'O Commander of the Faithful, we are in the sanctuary of God, Almighty and Great, and {God's contract (*ʿahd Allāh*)} is serious' (*History*, xviii/Morony. 186).

Humans are obligated by their primordial assent to worship none but God. However, in order for there to be moral choices, there must be temptation, and Iblis is the 'fallen' creature who tempts humans to worship themselves, or other humans, instead of God; in Tabari's words:

God had created Iblīs beautiful. He had ennobled him and honored him and reportedly made him ruler over the lower heaven and the earth. In addition, He had made him one of the keepers of Paradise. But he became overbearing toward his Lord and claimed divine lordship for himself and reportedly called on those under his control to worship him. Therefore, God transformed him into a stoned Satan. He deformed him and deprived him of the benefits He had granted him. He cursed him and drove him out of His heavens in the fleeting present world and then gave to him and his followers and partisans the Fire of Hell as their place of residence in the other world. We take refuge in God for protection against His divine wrath and against whatever action brings a person close to His wrath and against getting into trouble. (*History*, i/Rosenthal. 249; for more on Iblis, see 249–82)

According to Tabari, Iblis' actions are paradigmatic of those kings who violated God's covenant and made themselves objects of worship:

Now, let us speak about the one who was the first to be given royal authority and was shown favor by God but was ungrateful for it. Having denied God's divine Lordship, he was proud and overbearing towards his Lord and was therefore deprived by God of His divine favor and shamed and humiliated. We shall continue to mention those who adopted his ways and followed in his foot-steps and were therefore subjected by God to His divine revenge. Counted among the partisans of Iblīs, they were made to share his shame and humiliation. There were also their counterparts and successors among kings and messengers and prophets who obeyed their Lord and left praiseworthy memories. God willing, we shall mention them, too. (Ibid, 249)

In this passage, 'God's favours and blessings' and the responses of 'gratitude' or 'ingratitude' refer explicitly to 'royal authority'. God grants the king the power to govern, and in return he is obliged to rule according to the covenant (*mīthāq*) and the legal contract (*ʿahd*).

Further ahead in Tabari's mythological narrative, the paradigm of adhering to the covenant and the contract is illustrated for the first time by the first Persian king Oshahanj, who ruled in Mesopotamia. He instituted *masājid* ('places for worship'), the basic crafts including agriculture, and the law, based on the covenant pledge:

The Persians say that this Ōshahanj was born a king. His way of life and the way he administered his subjects were outstandingly praiseworthy. That gave rise to his surname Fēshdādh, which in Persian means 'the first to judge in justice' {…} he placed a crown (*tāj*) upon his head and gave an address in which he said that he had inherited the realm from his grandfather Jayūmart and that he meant (to inflict) punishment and revenge upon rebellious human beings and Satans. Again, they mention that he subdued Iblīs and his armies and forbade them to mix with human beings. Writing a document on a white sheet (*ṭirs*), he {took from them the covenant pledges (*akhadha ʿalayhim fīhi al-mawāthiq*)} enjoining them not to confront any human being. He threatened them in case they did. He killed the rebels among them and a number of ghūls ('demons'). (Ibid, 342)

The first human model (as opposed to Iblis) for the 'Satanic' king is also presented here in the mythological prelude, in the form of Biwarasb, or, in Arabic, al-Ḍaḥḥak. Tabari related that al-Dahhak resided in the Sawad, from where he ruled 'all the earth'. Whereas Oshahanj had instituted worship and justice based on the covenant, Biwarasb instituted the mint and taxation, as well as cruel punishments; the oppressiveness of his rule took monstrous proportions:

Al-Ḍaḥḥak reportedly reigned for one thousand years after Jam—but God knows better. Settling in the Sawād in a town called Nars near the Kūfah Road, he ruled over all the earth, displaying tyranny and oppression. He killed excessively and was the first to enact (the punishments of) crucifixion and mutilation. He was also the first to levy tithes and to mint dirhams, and the first to sing and be sung to. It is said that there were two ganglia growing out of his shoulders, which caused pain to him. The pain became so intense that he would anoint them with the brains of human beings. For this purpose he killed two men each day and anointed his ganglia with their brains. When he did this, the pain would abate. (*History*, ii/Brinner. 3–4)

According to another report, al-Dahhak was eventually killed by a hero from among the people; the weapon he used to kill the tyrant later became the banner of the Persian kings of Fars, who were just rulers.

Oshahanj's institutions (religious worship and the law) are thus described as in line with the mythical covenant. Biwarasb's mint and tax, however, are portrayed as liable to abuse for oppression and tyranny. The conclusion is that worship of God and legal justice presuppose each other, and are the only way to ensure that money and taxation are not used to wrong people.

The mythological prelude continues by narrating God's wrath against humanity, and the Flood, which builds on the Biblical narrative about Noah and his sons. That is the point at which myth turns into 'proper history'.

ABRAHAM AND THE PILGRIMAGE

The destruction of the Ka'ba by the Flood marks the transition from mythical to 'real' history, which begins with Abraham's restoration of the Ka'ba and institutionalization of the pilgrimage with the details it was to have in the Islamic rites that, in due time, were instituted by the Prophet.

Abraham was born in the Sawad, and a worshipper of the One God. He fought fearlessly against Nimrod's idol-worshippers until he had to flee to Harran, and from there onwards to Egypt and Canaan. In Canaan, after the births of his sons Ishmael (Ismāʿīl) by Hagar and Isaac (Isḥāq) by Sarah, Abraham was commanded by God to go to Makka and build for Him a House 'in which [God] would be worshipped and His name mentioned' (ibid, 69). The reports about how Abraham built the Ka'ba together with his son Ishmael are numerous. When the building had been erected, Abraham re-institutionalized the pilgrimage rites after the precedent of Adam, but in a much more detailed way, describing the different stations and observances of the actual pilgrimage. The idea that the Ka'ba marks a physical meeting-point, where humans stand before God, was given expression in the call the pilgrims utter upon arrival at the Ka'ba: 'Here I am, my Lord, here I am! (*labbayka ya rabbī labbayk*).' (Ibid, 80)

As we saw, Tabari presented Persian kingship as the first ruling institution that was founded on the covenant, and Abraham as the prophet who institutionalized the precise ritual for annually celebrating the covenant. In this context, he also points ahead (ibid, 81–82) to the Prophet, who will be commanded by God to 'follow the religion of Abraham, as one upright by nature. He was not an idolater' (Q. 16. 123). As we shall see in due course, the Prophet is the one who restores both the covenant and its annual ritual.

MOSES' LAW

The covenant is the bare principle of entering into mutual and legally binding obligations and rights. This implies that it can take the form of many different positive laws, or contracts. In Tabari's *History*, the first prophet to give a positive law from God was Moses. The report about how God summoned Moses to be His prophet is from Ibn Ishaq and Ka'b al-Ahbar, the convert rabbi:

When the night came on which God wished to show His favor upon Moses and on which He started him on his prophethood and His speaking to him, Moses took the wrong road, so that he did not know where he was going. He took out his fire drill to kindle a fire for his family so that they might sleep around it and in the morning they would awaken and he could determine his path's direction. However, his fire drill became inert and would not strike a fire for him. He continued to strike it until, [when] it tired him, a fire glowed. When he saw it, '*he said to his family: Wait! Lo! I discern a fire. Perhaps I may bring you a brand from it or may find guidance at the fire*' {Q. 20. 10 …} So he moved toward it, and behold! it was in a creeping bush – although some among the scriptuaries say it was in a boxthorn. When he came near, it drew back from him. When he saw it draw back, he retreated from it, feeling a sense of fear. When he wanted to leave, it drew near him. Then something was spoken from the bush. When he heard the voice, he listened, and God said to him: '*Take off your shoes, for lo! you are in the holy valley of Ṭuwāʾ, and he threw them.*' (*History*, iii/Brinner. 50–1)

Tabari then related the Biblical narratives of Moses' struggle against Pharaoh, his leading the Israelites into the desert towards the Promised Land, and the sending down of the law to Moses on Mount Sinai, as described in a report from Ibn 'Abbas:

When God spoke to Moses, he desired to see Him and asked his Lord if he might look at Him. {…} Then God said to Moses: '*I have chosen you above mankind by My messages and by My speaking. So take what I have given you and be one of the thankful.*' {Q. 7. 143–4) …} And He said to him: '*What has made you hasten to go ahead of your people, O Moses?*' {Q. 20. 83} 'Then Moses went back to his people, angry and sad', {Q. 20. 86} *and with him was God's {contract} on his tablets* {*wa maʿahu ʿahdu l-lāhi fī alwāhihi*}. (Ibid, 76–7; emphasis added)

As giver of the law from God, Moses is the main prophetic model for the Prophet Muhammad.

THE LAND AND THE PERSIAN KINGS

The sources Tabari used for his reports on the Persian kings draw on two kinds of material: the Greek epic about Alexander the Great (the 'Alexander Romance') from the third century AD, and Sassanid king lists, which include material from the later parts of the Zoroastrian Avesta. The Sassanid king lists are organized according to a calendar which the founder of the dynasty, king Ardashir I (r. 226–41), had ordered from his Zoroastrian high priest Tansar. This was a straightforward adaptation of the lunar calendar used by Alexander's successors, the Greek Seleucids (360–323 BC), but modified so that the Seleucid year 0 (312 BC) coincided with the appearance of the Zoroastrian prophet Zoroaster in the Sassanid reckoning. Then, to adapt the calendar to events significant for the Sassanids, the king lists based on it arranged the kings so that there was a time span of 538 years between the appearance of Zoroaster and the ascent of king Ardashir to the throne in 226. The result was a slightly skewed chronology. Since Tabari used the Sassanid king lists as his main structure, his overall chronology reproduced its flaws.

The Persian king lists were contained in a Pahlavi (Middle Persian) text entitled *Khudāynāma* ('The history of the kings'), compiled in the reign of the last Sassanid king Yazdagird III (r. 632–51) and preserved in Arabic translations done by statesmen and historians specialized in Persian imperial administration, e.g. *Siyar muluk al-ᶜajam* by the Zoroastrian convert and statesman Ibn al-Muqaffaᶜ (d. 757). Tabari used these Arabic translations, and possibly also some Pahlavi sources. His sections on the Persian kings constitute the richest extant historical narrative about them.[1]

The terms covenant and contract occur in reports about both Persians and Israelites. However, the institutions and practices of the system of vassalage, the societal context of states and law, are described in the reports about the Persian kings. In these narratives, the Sawad lands and the province of Fars appear as discreet but persistent themes.

Among the pre-Sassanid kings, Manushihr plays an important part. In Tabari's chronology, he was contemporary with Moses. He fought the Turks and sought to expand the Persian empire through military power. He is also described as the king who initiated large-scale agriculture in the Sawad

---

[1] See Hildegard Lewy, 'The Genesis of the Faulty Persian Chronology'; Mohsen Zakeri, 'al-Tabari on Sasanian History'; Zeev Rubin, 'al-Tabari and the Age of the Sasanians'.

by constructing a system of irrigation canals; hence, in the reports about him, a connection between agriculture and financing the army is established. After initial Persian victories, the Turks recovered and seized some provinces from Manushihr's dominions. In this context, Tabari quotes a speech which the king gave and in which he echoes the theme of gratitude towards God:

{T}he Turks have seized a part of your outlying districts. That is only because you abandoned warfare against your enemy and you lacked concern. But God has granted us dominion as *a test of whether we will be grateful*, and he will increase us, or will disbelieve and He will punish us, though we belong to a family of renown, for the source of rule belongs to God. (Ibid, 24–5; italics added)

That gratitude towards God has concrete implications for how the king should govern is illustrated in another speech by Manushihr to an assembly consisting of the Zoroastrian High Priest (*Mōbadh mōbadhan*), members of the royal family, and military commanders from the nobility. Here the king spells out the connection between the covenant principle to worship none but God, and the king's entering into mutually binding, contractual obligations with his subjects:

Verily God has given us this dominion, and to Him belongs praise. We ask Him to inspire us with integrity, truth, and certainty. For the king has a claim on his subjects, and his subjects have a claim on him, whereas their obligation to the ruler is that they obey him, give him good counsel, and fight his enemy; the king's obligation to them is to provide them with their sustenance in its proper times, for they cannot rely on anything else, and that is their commerce. The king's obligation to his subjects is that he take care of them, treat them kindly, and not impose on them what they cannot do. If a calamity befalls them and diminishes their gains because a heavenly or earthly evil comes upon them, he should deduct from the land tax that which was diminished. If a calamity ruins them altogether, he should give them what they need to strengthen their rebuilding. Afterward, he may take from them to the extent that he does not harm them, for a year or two years. (Ibid, 25–6)

From the point of view of the system of vassalage, it should be noted that the land tax is the focus around which the mutual obligations of the king and his subjects are defined. In a later part of the speech the function of land tax as sustenance of the army is brought in too:

The relationship of the army to the king is of the same status as the two wings of a bird, for they are the wings of the king. Whenever a feather is cut off from a wing, that is a blemish in it. Likewise in the case of the king, for he is equally dependent on his wings and feathers. Moreover, the king must possess three qualities: first, that he be truthful and not lie, that he be bountiful and not be miserly, and that he be in control of himself in anger, for he is given power with his hand outstretched and the land tax coming to him. He must not appropriate to himself what belongs to his troops and his subjects. (Ibid, 26)

The speech is concluded by Manushihr emphasizing the causal connection between the king's justice and the amount of land tax revenue and, dependent on that, the relative strength of the military:

Know that this dominion will not stand except through uprightness and good obedience, suppression of the enemy, blocking the frontiers, justice to the subjects, and just treatment of the oppressed. Your healing is within you; the remedy in which there is no illness is uprightness, commanding good and forbidding evil. For there is no power except in God. Look to the subjects, for they are your food and drink. Whenever you deal justly with them, they desire prosperity, which will increase your land-tax revenues and will be made evident in the growth of your wealth. But, if you wrong the subjects, they will abandon cultivation and leave most of the land idle. This will decrease your land-tax revenues, and it will be made evident in the decrease of your wealth. Pledge yourself to deal justly with your subjects. (Ibid, 27)

Manushihr is thus presented as the first example in 'real' history of 'the good-king-model' set by the mythical king Ôshahanj. The speech seems to address the concerns of

Tabari and the administrators of his day: how to strike a balance between the state's need for tax revenue to pay the army and not over-taxing the peasants and merchants.

The system of vassalage in its concrete form of provinces, irrigation canals, and tax collection, was institutionalized by another renowned Persian fighter against the Turks, Kay Qubadh: '[H]e assigned the river and spring waters for irrigating the lands. He gave names to the lands, determined their boundaries, set up provinces, and clarified the divisions of each province and its territory. He commanded the people to take the land, and collected a tithe from its produce to provision the army.' (Ibid, 116–17)

The examples above are taken from mythological and ancient Persian dynasties. There are others from narratives about the historical Sassanid dynasty (226–651). A specific model of taxation is described in the narrative about Khusraw Anushirwan (r. 531–79) and his reforms based on a new land and population survey in the empire. The source of this report was the Zoroastrian convert and statesman Ibn al-Muqaffaʿ (d. 757) and his *Siyar muluk al-ʿajam* (see above, p. 84). Tabari relates that, before Khusraw's reform, the Persian kings had instituted a system of sharecropping (*muqāsama*) where the landlord determined the land tax (*kharāj*) case by case, depending on water supply, area of cultivation, and size of harvest, and supplemented it with a fixed poll tax. While it appears just to tax actual produce rather than levy a fixed percentage, *muqāsama* in practice subjected peasants to the arbitrary estimations of landlords, who often made no allowances at all for destroyed or diminished crops. Moreover, landlords tended to withhold collected revenue from the state treasury, with the resulting endemic problem of the state losing control over the provinces and the military. Khusraw's reform retained the poll-tax and instituted a land tax based on cultivable area and crop estimates, which was assessed and collected by the state administration (not by landlords). The fixed rates and payment in three instalments both ensured a predictable, steady income for the state and protected the peasants against extortion. The reforms also specified exemptions from both land and poll tax in cases of hardship:[1]

Kisrā {Khusraw} chose some men of sound judgement and wise counsel, and ordered them to investigate the various types of crops the cadastral survey had revealed for him, the numbers of date palms and olive trees, and the numbers of heads of those liable for the poll tax. On that basis, they were to fix the rates of taxation by the yardsticks of what they perceived would ensure the well-being of his subjects and ample means of sustenance for them. They were to report the results of this to him. {...}

Kisrā ordered the new tax assessments to be written down in several copies. One copy was to be kept in his own chancery close at his hand; one copy was sent to the land-tax collectors (*ʿummal al-kharāj*) for them to collect taxes on its basis; and another copy was sent to the judges of the administrative divisions (*quḍāt al-kuwar*). The judges were charged with the duty of intervening between the tax collectors and the people if the tax collectors in the administrative districts attempted to raise an additional sum above the amount laid down in the master copy of the tax assessment in the chancery, of which they had received a copy. Also, the judges were to exempt from land tax those whose tillage or other tax-attracting produce had been damaged or badly affected in any way, according to the seriousness of that damage or defect. Regarding those persons liable for the poll tax who had died, or who had passed the age fifty, collecting the taxation was likewise suspended; the judges were to write back to Kisrā about the tax exemptions here, which they had granted so that Kisrā might issue appropriate instructions to his tax collectors. Furthermore, the judges were not to let the tax collectors levy taxation on persons aged less than twenty. (*History*, v/Bosworth. 257, 261–2)

The tax reform was accompanied by a reform of the army. Tabari relates how, before Khusraw, there was only

---

[1] On Khusraw's reforms, see also: Rubin, 'The Reforms'; Frye, *History of Ancient Iran*, 324 *et passim.*

one army commander (Pers. *ispahbadh*) for the entire empire, but he divided the empire into four regional commands, each with an administrator in charge of reviewing army affairs. Also, he improved equipment and established elite cavalry units. Khusraw thereby managed to re-conquer provinces which had come under the control of regional monarchs. In the long run, however, it seems revenues did not suffice, so commanders were assigned villages for tax-farming, which gave rise to a new class of small military landowners (Ar. *asāwira*). In addition, Turkish peoples on the eastern and Arabs on the south-western frontiers challenged Sassanid power. Tabari here points out that so long as Khusraw upheld justice – i.e. upheld God's covenant – his empire withstood its enemies:

{...} news reached Kisrā that a band of Turkish youths had raided the furthest boundaries of his land. He ordered his ministers and provincial governors not to go beyond what was just in the course of their official duties and not to act in any way during the course of those duties except justly. Because of this policy of acting justly, God deflected that enemy from Kisra's land without him having to make war on them or undertake great trouble in repelling them. (Ibid, 265)

The analysis of Khusraw's government appears to stop short in the reference to God's power, but, just as in Manushihr's speech, the connection is made between God's sustaining an empire and the king's adherence to legal principles regulating land tax. In terms of historical causality, it is the human actions which drive events.

Tabari ends his account of Khusraw Anushirwan by stating that the Messenger of God was born in his reign. On the night of his birth, Khusraw's palace shook, and several other omens occurred, all of which signified that Arabs would seize the Persian empire. Khusraw died shortly after these events and was succeeded by his son Hurmuz (r. 579–90). Tabari portrays Hurmuz as a well-intentioned populist who tried to court 'the commoners' by getting tough with the landed nobility and the priesthood:

He removed the nobles [from his court and entourage] and killed 13,600 men from the religious classes and from those of good family and noble birth. His sole aim was to win over the lower classes and to make them favorably disposed towards him. He imprisoned a great number of the great men, and degraded them and stripped them of their offices and ranks. He provide{d} well for the mass of the troops (*al-jund*), but deprived the cavalrymen of their resources. Hence a great number of those in his entourage became evil intentioned toward him, as a consequence of the fact that God wished to change their [i.e., the Persians'] rule and transfer their royal power to someone else. Everything has its own particular cause. (Ibid, 297–8)

Hurmuz's policy undermined the elite cavalry that Khusraw Anushirwan had set up. Just as God sustained Khusraw's empire so long as he ruled justly, God transferred Sassanid power to the Arabs on account of Hurmuz's erroneous politics.

Hurmuz was succeeded by his son Khusraw Parviz (591–628). Here Tabari synchronized Persian political decline with the Prophet's *hijra* to Madina, which marks the transformation of the Muslim community into a proper society and state. The correlation between Persian imperial decline and the emergence of Islam is also evident in the following report from Ibn Ishaq:

Kisrā constructed a dam on the 'Blind Tigris' (*Dijla al-ʿAwrāʾ*) and expended on it sums of such magnitude that no one knew their extent. {…} Now when God sent His Prophet Muḥammad, Kisrā woke up one morning and found that the arched roof of his royal palace (*ṭāq mulkihi*) had collapsed in the middle without any weight having been put upon it; also, that the [dam on the] 'Blind Tigris' had been breached. When he saw all that, he became filled with grief and said, '{…}*Shah bishikast*', meaning [in Arabic] 'the king has been overthrown (literally, "broken").' Then he summoned his soothsayers, magicians, and astrologers, and summoned al-Sāʾib with them, too. He told them {…} 'Look into this matter and see exactly what it is.' {…} Al-Sāʾib spent the whole of a dark, overcast night on a hillock, where he saw a lightning flash that arose from the direction of the Ḥijāz, flew across the heavens, and reached as far as the East. The next morning, he looked at what was beneath his feet, and behold, there was a green meadow. He then made a pronouncement in his role as diviner: 'If what I was seeing is true, there will arise from Ḥijāz a dominion (*sulṭān*) which will reach the East and from which the earth will grow green and fertile – much more so than from any previous kingdom.' (Ibid, 331–2)

The earth become 'green and fertile' mentioned in the last sentence symbolizes cultivated land as the mainstay of empire; the breaching of the dam, which served the purpose of irrigating the land, is a symbolical way of saying that Khusraw had lost his empire. The omen is followed by accounts of political developments leading up to the Battle of Dhu Qar, the first Arab victory over the Sassanids. The battle occurred because Khusraw Parviz had violated his part of the contract with his Arab vassal, al-Nuʿman b. al-Mundhir, and brought about the latter's death; Tabari comments: '{he} died at Khāniqīn, just a short while before the coming of Islam. Soon afterward, God sent His prophet; al-Nuʿmān's fate was the cause of the battle of Dhu Qar.' (Ibid, 358; see also 352–8)

But there were other causes also. The nobility rose against Khusraw Parviz, and he was eventually brought to trial on a catalogue of charges, including 'what you have inflicted on your subjects generally in levying the land tax and in treating them with harshness and violence; [and] your amassing a great amount of wealth, which you extracted from the people with great brutality so that you drove them to consider your rule hateful and thereby brought them into affliction and deprivation' (ibid, 383). Tabari reports Khusraw Parviz's self-defence in the form of a speech to his prosecutors that gives a very precise account of the system of vassalage and the logic of taxation and military power:

Know, O ignorant one, that after God, it is only wealth and troops that can uphold the royal authority of monarchs, this being especially the case with the kingdom of Persia, whose lands are surrounded by enemies {...}. The only thing that can keep them from it {...} is numerous troops and copious quantities of weapons and war material. {...} these can only be acquired by having a great deal of wealth and ample quantities of it; and wealth can only be amassed and gathered together, for any contingency which may arise, by strenuous efforts and dedication in levying this land tax. We are not the first ones to have gathered together wealth; on the contrary, we have merely imitated here our forefathers and our predecessors in past times. They collected wealth just as we have, and amassed great quantities of it, so that it might constitute a firm backing for them in strengthening their armies, in upholding their authority, and in [making possible] other things for which wealth must inevitably be amassed. (Ibid, 392)

To sum up this section on the Persian kings, we have seen that they instituted the system of vassalage and, within its terms, the social contract defining mutual obligations and rights. Tabari describes a specific tax system adapted to the needs of the state in his account of Khusraw Anushirwan's taxation and army reforms. He also gives several historical examples of what happened when contractual obligations and rights were violated, i.e. when 'reason' was abandoned. Anushirwan's tax reforms, centralizing collection and redistribution under state administration while protecting the basic needs of the peasants, is described as a model which can strengthen the state. This is also emphasized in the report about the good king Manushihr and his social contract. Now, the 'Abbasid standard tax model, introduced by the caliph al-Mahdi (r. 775–85), was *muqāsama*, i.e. similar to the one Khusraw had changed because it left everything in the hands of the vassals. Tabari's acquaintance, 'the good vizier' 'Ali b. 'Isa, seems to have centralized tax levying and collection in the same manner as illustrated in the *History* by Anushirwan. 'Ali b. 'Isa also kept down tax pressure by avoiding costly war campaigns against Byzantium and the

Isma'ilis; by comparison, Khusraw Parviz illustrates the connection between expansionist war against Byzantium and oppressive taxation. It is therefore tempting to suggest that the account of Khusraw's successful, 'rational' government serves to illustrate the potential benefits of 'Ali b. 'Isa's policy.

THE PROPHET'S MISSION AND STATE

The Prophet lived between 570 and 632. In Tabari's narrative, reports about the early part of the Prophet's life, i.e. his birth and childhood, are woven into the main narrative about Khusraw Anushirwan (*History*, vol. 5), and the turning-point of the Hijra located in the reign of Khusraw Parviz. The narrative about his adult life (vols. 6–9), however, represents a distinct structure with a single focus on the Prophet and the Muslim community as historical actors. It is divided into two parts: his early life and prophetic mission in Makka (570–622), and his years as head of state in Madina (622–32), the Hijra marking the transition between the two periods. Here is not the place to go into the details of the Prophet's life, only to show where it fits within Tabari's preoccupation with covenant and contract.

That side of the significance of the Prophet's mission is best understood in relation to tribal organization. The basic building block of tribal society was the extended family, related through first cousin marriage. Extended families formed coalitions (tribes), often but not always related by blood. Each family was headed by a *shaykh* or 'elder', who represented its interests in relation to the other families in the tribe. Consensus was the aim; if it could not be reached, severe feuds could break out between families. The tribe sometimes entered vassal treaties, putting its warriors at the service of kings. The virtues celebrated by the pre-Islamic Arabs of the Hijaz centred on the heroic warrior and his indomitable personality, accompanied by intense pride in the family genealogy and its honour. The Prophet's tribe Quryash had been vassals of the Sassanids (*Jami'*, vol. v., 6.121, 22). However, there was in the Hijaz no central state with a regular military, administration, and law which the tribes were obliged to submit to. This is reflected in the fact that tribal culture was largely *oral* and its law customary; the absence of a state bureaucracy meant that there was little need for written contracts and documents.

Religious life on the Arabian Peninsula at the time was complex, and had been so since at least the fourth century AD, when the Peninsula became increasingly drawn into the power struggle between the Byzantine and Sassanid empires. The presence of Jews in Arabia dates from at least the destruction of the Jerusalem Temple by the Romans in 70 AD, and possibly the Babylonian exile in 586 BC. Zoroastrianism, the state religion of the Sassanids, entered Arabia both from Mesopotamia and south Arabia. In the late fourth century, southern Arabia came under the rule of the Arian Christian kingdom of Abyssinia, and Arian missions took hold there. Nestorianism and Monophysitism spread from Mesopotamia and Syria, from the Sassanid and Byzantine Arab vassal kingdoms of Ghassan and Lakhm, from the fifth century onwards. Tabari's narrative of these Arab kingdoms is interwoven with the history of Persian kingships (*History*, vols. 4 and 5).

Tabari pays only scant attention to religious matters, as his interest was with politics. He mentions that the Quraysh worshiped the gods Hubal, al-Lat and al-'Uzza, and that the goddess Manat was worshipped in Yathrib (*History*, vi/Watt & McDonald. 107, 110–11, 120; vii/McDonald & Watt, 187–8). The Prophet's family, Banu Hashim, were in charge of 'polytheistic' pilgrimage to the Ka'ba. There are also a few references to members of the Quraysh who had converted to Christianity, notably Waraqa b. Nawfal, cousin of the Prophet's wife Khadija. Judaism or, rather, Jews, are frequently mentioned in the narratives about the Prophet's career as head of state in Madina (vols. 6–9).

Tabari's reports tell us that the Arabs had once known the One God and His covenant, and its ritual celebration at the Ka'ba sanctuary, as instituted by Abraham. However, they had forgotten it and begun to worship statues of other gods in human form; the Prophet's mission is therefore to remind them. The Prophet's lineage is traced through Ishmael, ancestor of the Arabs, to Abraham, who restored the Ka'ba after the Flood and instituted the pilgrimage rituals, and from him back all the way to Adam, the first to found the Ka'ba and circle it in veneration of God. When the Quraysh undertook to repair the Ka'ba, the future Prophet Muhammad was given the honour of putting the stone which God had thrown down from Paradise back in its place (*History*, vi/Watt & McDonald. 51–9).

The Prophet's mission began when, at the age of forty, he received his first revelation from God, transmitted by the Archangel Gabriel. In a regular practice of penitence, he had wandered out of the city to the desolate mountains around Makka, leaving his family in a 'base camp' while he proceeded to a cave in Mount Hira' for solitary reflection. Many of the details in the report about what followed link the event to the report about the revelation to Moses ('When the night came', see above p. 82):

When the month came in which God willed to ennoble him, in the year in which God made him His Messenger, this being the month of Ramadan, the Messenger of God went out as usual to Ḥirāʾ accompanied by his family. When the night came on which God ennobled him by making him His Messenger and thereby showed mercy on His servants, Gabriel brought him the command of God. The Messenger of God said, 'Gabriel came to me as I was sleeping with a brocade cloth in which was writing. He said, "{Read}!", and I said, "I cannot {read}." He pressed me tight and almost stifled me, until I thought I would die. Then he let me go,

and said, "{Read}!" I said, "What shall I {read}?" only saying that in order to free myself from him, fearing that he might repeat what he had done to me. He said:
"{Read} in the name of your Lord who creates! He creates man from a clot of blood. {Read}: And your Lord is the Most Bountiful, He who teaches by the pen, teaches man what he knew not." {Q. 96. 1–5}
I recited it, and then he desisted and departed. I woke up, and it was as though these words had been written on my heart.' (Ibid, 70–1)

The report then describes how the Prophet, profoundly shaken, hurried back to Khadija and told her what had happened. She believed in him and comforted him; later she reported his experience to her cousin, Waraqa b. Nawfal, a convert to Christianity who 'read the Scriptures, and learned from the people of the Torah and the Gospel', what the Prophet had told her (ibid, 72). When the Prophet had returned to Makka and was circling the Ka'ba, he met Waraqa who asked him to retell his story. He heard it and said: 'By Him in whose hand is my soul, you are the prophet of this community, and there has come to you the greatest Nāmūs, he who came to Moses {*wa laqad jāʾaka al-nāmūs al-akbar alladhī jāʾa ilā Mūsā*}.' (Ibid)

Nāmūs is an Arabic rendering of Greek *nomos*, 'law'; what came to both Messengers was the law. Clearly, the Prophet is presented as the heir to Moses specifically as the giver of the law and its corollary, the *written* contract. Accordingly, the opening word in the first revelation from God (cited above) was *iqraʾ* ('read'), from the same root (*q-r-ʾ*) as 'the Qur'an', 'the reading'.

Tabari's narrative draws a parallel between opposition from the Prophet's tribe, the Quraysh, and the recalcitrance of the Israelites before Moses. The Quraysh had no intention of abandoning their many gods for Muhammad's One God. However, religious sentiment was only one side of their opposition. Tabari presents a report which shows another, political, concern. The Prophet's uncle Abu Talib, anxious to mediate between his nephew and the mighty of Quraysh, gathered an assembly:

Abū Ṭālib sent for the Messenger of God, and when he came in he said, 'Nephew, here are the shaykhs and nobles of your tribe. They have asked for justice against you, that you should desist from reviling their gods and they will leave you to your God.' 'Uncle,' he said, 'shall I not summon them to something which is better for them than their gods?' 'What do you summon them to?' he asked. He replied, 'I summon them to utter a saying through which the Arabs will submit to them and they will rule over the non-Arabs.' Abū Jahl said from among the gathering, 'What is it, by your father? We will give you it and ten like it.' He answered, 'That you should say, "There is no god but God."' They took fright at that and said, 'Ask for anything rather than that!' But he said, 'If you were to bring me the sun and put it into my hand, I would not ask you for anything other than this.'

They rose up to leave in anger and said, 'By God, we shall revile you and your God who commands you to do this!' (Ibid, 95)

The political implication of 'the Arabs will submit to them and they will rule over the non-Arabs' – a prophecy of future conquests of Byzantine and Sassanid territories – is that Quraysh must submit to the Messenger's single authority. This represented a centralization of power under one leader, typical of monarchic states and different from Qurayshi tribal organization, with its celebration of independence, family glory and honour. Thus the Quraysh were rejecting, as well as monotheism, a new political organization.

It is in this context in Tabari's *History* that his notorious report from Ibn Ishaq about the 'Satanic verses' is found. The Quraysh, increasingly worried by the slow but steady stream of converts to the worship of the One God, continued to turn away from the Prophet's message:

When the Messenger of God saw how his tribe turned their backs on him and was grieved to see them shunning the message he had brought to them from God, he longed in his soul that something would come to him from God which would reconcile him with his tribe. With his love for his tribe and his eagerness for their welfare it would have delighted him if some of the difficulties which they made for him could have been smoothed out, and he debated with himself and fervently desired such an outcome. Then God revealed:

'By the Star when it sets, your comrade does not err, nor is he deceived; nor does he speak out of (his own) desire …' {Q. 53. 1–3} and when he came to the words:

'Have you thought upon al-Lāt and al-ʿUzzā and Manāt, the third, the other?' {Q. 53. 19–20}

Satan cast on his tongue, because of his inner debates and what he desired to bring to his people, the words:

'These are the high-flying cranes; verily their intercession is accepted with approval.'

When Quraysh heard this, they rejoiced and were happy and delighted at the way in which he spoke of their gods, and they listened to him, while the Muslims, having complete trust in their Prophet in respect of the messages which he brought from God, did not suspect him of error, illusion, or mistake. {…} Then Gabriel came to the Messenger of God and said, 'Muḥammad, what have you done? You have recited to the people that which I did not bring to you from God, and you have said that which was not said to you.' Then the Messenger of God was much grieved and feared God greatly, but God sent down a revelation to him, for He was merciful to him, consoling him and making the matter light for him, informing him that there had never been a prophet or messenger before him who desired as he desired and wished as he wished but that Satan had cast words into his recitation, as he had cast words on Muḥammad's tongue. Then God cancelled what Satan had thus cast, and established his verses by telling him that he was like other prophets and messengers, and revealed:

'Never did We send a messenger or a prophet before you but that when he recited (the Message) Satan cast words into his recitation (*umniyyah*). God abrogates what Satan casts. Then God established His verses. God is knower, wise.' {Q. 22. 52} (Ibid, 108–9)

This is a remarkable example of how Ibn Ishaq's reports make the Prophet the embodiment of all prophets; as God said, satanic temptation is a standard element in all prophetic missions; the best known case being Jesus in the desert.

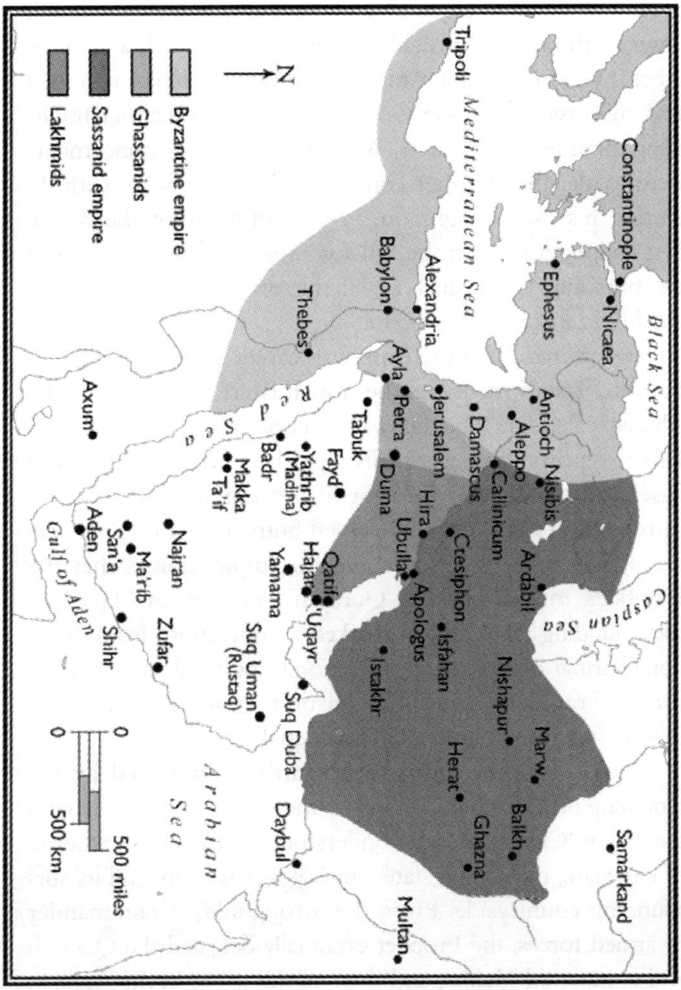

Map 4. *Arabia on the eve of Islam; the Byzantine and Sassanid empires and the territories of their vassals, the Ghassan and Lakhm tribes*

After that incident, the Quraysh became violently hostile towards the Prophet and the believers. The institution of the societal and political dimensions of the Prophet's message could not be realized in Makka. In Yathrib, an agricultural town to the north of Makka, inhabited by Jewish and Arab tribes, two long-feuding Arab tribes, 'Aws and Khazraj, hoped that submission to One God under one commander might bring them peace and unity. When the necessary arrangements were made, the Prophet commanded the Hijra to Yathrib. During his own emigration, in the company of the future first caliph, Abu Bakr, he hid for three days in a cave from the pursuing Quraysh; a detail mirroring how the Biblical David hid in a cave from Saul.

Before narrating the Prophet's career as head of state in Yathrib, Tabari mentions the (much later) institution of the Islamic calendar. The Hijra was chosen as starting point, Tabari reports, because it 'distinguished between truth and falsehood' (ibid, 158). In light of the statement in Tabari's Introduction that God has blessed humans so that they may distinguish truth and falsehood, the implication is that the Prophet's migration from Qurayshi 'idolatry' in Makka to state-building in Yathrib marked a transition from 'irrational' tribal organization to 'rational' political organization and government based on a constitution and a written law, before which each individual was equal.

That transition seems to be further underlined by the renaming of Yathrib as *al-Madīna*, 'the City', concurrently with the Hijra. 'City' should be understood in the classical sense of city state, meaning a state which governs a city and its surrounding countryside. From this stronghold, as commander of armed forces, the Prophet eventually defeated the Quraysh and conquered Makka, and then all the tribes in the Arabian Peninsula submitted to his rule. Those who were Jewish or Christian had to accept a contract of allegiance and protection with the state of the Messenger of God (*History*, vols. 8–9). Thus, within the Prophet's lifetime Madina expanded into something more than the classical city state. It was to prove the stepping-stone to an Arab empire.

THE MADINA CALIPHATE AND THE CONQUESTS

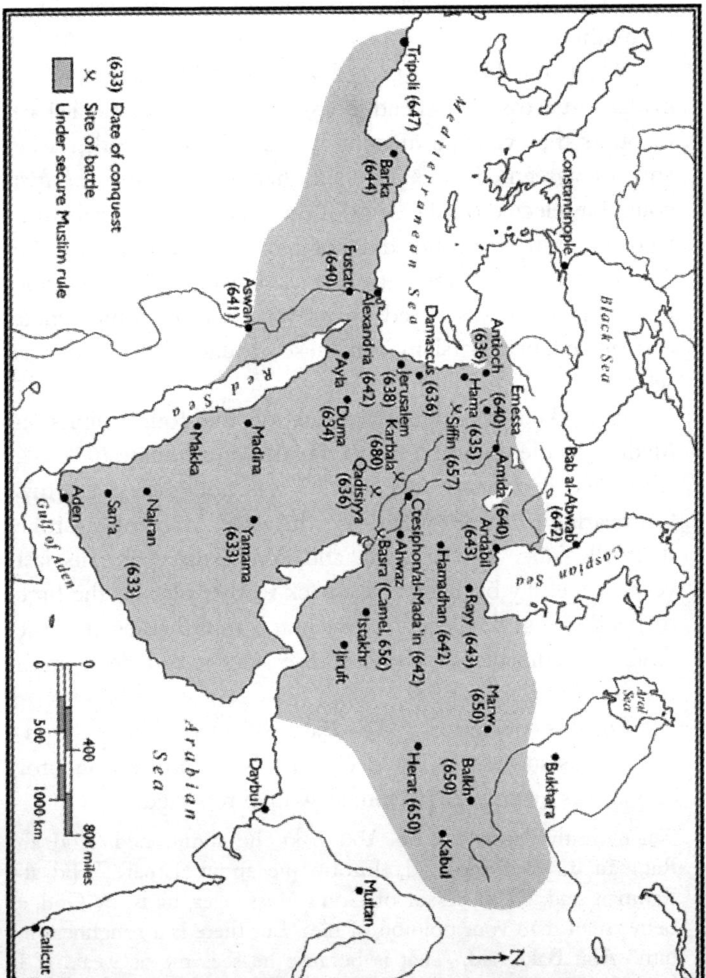

Map 5. *Expansion of territories under Muslim rule during the Companion caliphates: and the sites of important battles*

Tabari's narratives about the Companion caliphs in Madina carry the issue of rational government into Islamic history.

The selection below illustrates this issue, and shows Tabari's position on the status of the four first caliphs, which is important to answer the question of his possible Shi'i sympathies.

When the Prophet passed away in 632, there was no evident successor as head of state. Therefore, as Tabari recounts the events, a meeting was held to debate the issue and an agreement was reached that a successor (*khalīfa*) could be selected on the basis of merit and dynastic relationship. Since the Prophet did not have a surviving son, the dynastic principle was reflected as kinship with his tribe Quraysh; merit was based on personal virtue, competence, and precedence in Islam. On these grounds Abu Bakr was selected.

Abu Bakr was the only one of the four caliphs in Madina to die a natural death. His short caliphate (632–34, recounted in *History*, vols. 10–11) was nonetheless stormy. On hearing of the Prophet's death, some Arab tribes broke their allegiance to the state, and Abu Bakr spent his last years forcefully bringing them back to the fold. By the time of his death in 634, this had been accomplished so that the Arabian Peninsula was back to the state it had been upon the death of the Prophet.

On his deathbed, Abu Bakr selected 'Umar b. al-Khattab as successor. The decision was not an easy one, for 'Umar was a complex person; al-Waqidi reported:

When death descended on Abū Bakr, he summoned ʿAbd al-Raḥmān b. 'Awf and said, 'Inform me about ʿUmar.' ʿAbd al-Raḥmān said, 'O successor of God's Messenger, he is, by God, a better man than your opinion of him. But there is a roughness in him.' Abū Bakr said, 'That is because he sees me as weak. If I entrust him with the affair, he will leave behind much of his present behaviour. O Abū Muḥammad, I have done it in haste. It appears to me, if I get angry at the man for something, he shows me his concurrence about it, but if I ease up towards him, he shows me vehemence over it. Do not mention, O Abū

Muḥammad, anything of what I have said to you.' ʿAbd al-Raḥmān said, 'Of course.'

Then Abū Bakr summoned ʿUthmān b. ʿAffān and said, 'O Abū 'Abdallāh, inform me about ʿUmar.' ʿUthmān responded, 'You are better informed about him.' Abū Bakr said, 'Let me decide that, O Abū ʿAbdallāh.' ʿUthmān said, 'O God, my knowledge about him is that what he does in private is better than what he shows openly, and there is no one like him among us.' Abū Bakr said, 'May God have mercy on you, O Abū ʿAbdallāh. Do not mention anything that I have mentioned to you.' {…} (*History*, xi/Blankinship. 146)

In the end, Abu Bakr made up his mind and had 'Uthman b. 'Affan write a document in which he designated 'Umar b. al-Khattab as his successor. It was 'Umar (r. 634–44) who took the historically decisive step of expanding the Prophet's state into an Islamic empire.

'Umar's caliphate is the most extensively treated of all in Tabari's *History*; in fact, 'Umar gets almost as much space as the Prophet, and the reports about him are loaded with royal and messianic symbolism (*History*, x. 145–225; xii–xiv). The conquests of Byzantine and Sassanid territories were accomplished under his direction; here we will concentrate on the Sassanid lands. The following report is set in the context of preparations for the Battle of al-Qadisiyya in 636, where 'Umar's armies, commanded by Sa'd b. Abi Waqqas, decisively defeated the Sassanids and conquered the Sawad. Sa'd is urging his troops to go ahead, and explicitly referred to the Sawad as 'the promised land':

On that day Saʿd [b. Abī Waqqāṣ] addressed those who were under his command. It was on a Monday in the month of Muḥarram in the year 14 {…}. Having praised God and extolled Him, he said: 'God is the Truth. He has no partner in His dominion and His words will never go unfulfilled. God has said: 'For We have written in the Psalms, after the Remembrance, "The earth shall be the inheritance of My righteous servants." ' {Q. 21. 105} This land is your inheritance and the promise of your Lord {*inna hādha mirāthakum wa mawʿūd rabbikum*}. (*History*, xii/Friedmann. 84)

By conquering these lands, 'Umar's caliphate established the material foundation of the Islamic empire, and through the Sassanid defeat in al-Qadisiyya, effectively inherited the mantle of Persian kingship. Tabari had made an explicit connection between 'Umar and Khusraw Anushriwan in his account of the latter's tax reform, which 'Umar was said to follow:

It was these tax assessments ʿUmar b. al-Khaṭṭāb followed when he conquered the Persian lands and levied taxation on the 'protected peoples' (*ahl al-dhimmah*) there, except that he levied taxation on every uncultivated (*ghāmir*) piece of land according to its potential yield, at the same rate as he levied on sown land. Also, he levied on every *jarīb* of land growing wheat or barley from one to two additional *qafīz*s of wheat; this he used for feeding his army. But in the specific case of Iraq, ʿUmar did not make any arrangements contrary to those of Kisrā regarding the *jarīb*s of land and regarding the date palms, olive trees, and the heads [of those liable to the poll tax], and he excluded from liability to taxation the people's means of daily sustenance, as Kisrā had done. (*History*, v/Bosworth. 260–1)

The connection between 'Umar and Khusraw acquires special significance if we think about it in terms of Tabari's presumed preference for 'Ali b. 'Isa's policy: Khusraw and 'Umar ruled successfully because of their rational tax system and just redistribution; hence they serve in the *History* as two examples of the benefits of the centralized *misāha* system.

According to Tabari, it was 'Umar who instituted the Islamic calendar. The need for it arose in response to the practicalities of imperial government and administration:

A money order {*sakk*} was brought before 'Umar which fell due in (the month of) Shaʿbān. 'Umar said: 'Which Shaʿbān? The one which is coming or the one we are in now?' Then he said to the Messenger of God's Companions, 'Contrive something for the people which they can recognize.' {…} In the end they agreed that they should see how long the Messenger of God had remained in al-Madinah. They found this to be ten years, and the era was reckoned from the Messenger of God's emigration. (*History*, vi/Watt & McDonald. 158)

Dating money orders was only one of the problems. Another, also needing a universally agreed calendar to resolve it was the issue of precedence (*sābiqa*) in Islam, on the basis of which land allocations or stipends from the state register were determined. 'Umar is quoted as saying: '[It is] a man's achievement in Islam, his precedence in Islam, his usefulness in Islam, and his need [that count]' (*History*, xiv/Smith. 118). Determining merit by belonging in Islam rather than by tribal affiliation is part of the shift towards rational state administration. In the following report, the new calendar is contrasted with the customary ways of dating of 'the descendants of Ishmael', i.e. the Arab tribes:

The account given by ᶜAlī b. Mujāhid narrated from his authorities for the chronology of the descendants of Ishmael is not far from the truth, which is that it was not their custom to date from an established (and well-known) event which the majority of them could adopt, but that, when they dated an event, they did so from (a local happening, such as) a drought which took place in some part of their country, a barren year which befell them, the reign of a governor who ruled over them, or an event the news of which became widespread among them. This is shown by the way in which their poets differ in their dating; if they had had a dating from an established event and a generally adopted basis, this difference among them would not have arisen. (*History*, vi/Watt & McDonald. 160)

The 'wide reach' of the imperial state thus went together with a universal calendar, and the objectivity and generality of the written law, as opposed to the 'local' tribal chronology, customs and oral agreements. Other distinctions (and points of future conflict) in the new imperial state concerned tribal loyalty to family and kin, as opposed to the state's need for professionals who put the state's interests before those of kin; 'merit', as an abstract principle detached from kinship, is thus associated with rational government and administration.

In Tabari's presentation, 'Umar succeeded not only to Persian but also Israelite messianic kingship. This is expressed in the symbolism contained in reports about his conquest, from the Byzantines, of Jerusalem and the Temple Mount, the place from where the Messiah is expected to re-establish the glorious and virtuous rule of David and Solomon. The Byzantines had forbidden Jews to ascend the Mount, and had, according to Tabari, desecrated it. Now, since the Messiah is supposed to enter Jerusalem on a donkey, Tabari makes a special point about 'Umar's riding beasts:

All in all 'Umar went to Syria four times. The first time he rode a horse; the second time he rode a camel; the third time he failed to reach Syria because the plague was raging, and the fourth time he entered Syria on a donkey. (*History*, xii/Friedmann. 188)

In this narrative, Tabari reports that 'Umar was twice halted by Jews who recognized him as the true Messiah. As further signs of his identity, 'Umar performed specific acts on the Temple Mount related to the prophet-king David: he located 'David's prayer direction (*mihrāb*)' and prayed there the Muslim dawn prayer (ibid, 194); he also started cleaning away the rubbish which defiled the place on the Mount where Solomon's Temple had stood. The former rabbi Ka'b al-Ahbar reported that 'Umar's advent and purification of the Mount was foretold by a prophet during the period of Roman hegemony in the first century AD:

The Byzantines (*Rūm*) attacked the sons of Israel, were given victory over them, and buried the temple. Then they were given another victory, but they did not attend to the temple until the Persians attacked them. The Persians oppressed the sons of Israel. Later the Byzantines were given victory over the Persians. Then you came to rule. God sent a prophet to the [city buried in] rubbish and said: 'Rejoice O Jerusalem (*Ūrī shalam*)! Al-Fārūq will come to you and cleanse you.' Another prophet was sent to Constantinople. He stood on a hill belonging to the city and said: 'O Constantinople, what did your people do to My House? They ruined it, presented you as if you were similar to My throne and made interpretations contrary to My purpose [...].' (Ibid, 196)

The honorific 'al-Fārūq' (meaning 'the one who distinguishes between truth and falsehood') was used in reference to 'Umar in other contexts as well (ibid, 189). To be able to distinguish between truth and falsehood is the hallmark of rationality, as Tabari stated in his Introduction, and the precondition for justice. This is clearly expressed in the following report, in the context of preparations for the Battle of al-Qadisiyya against the Sassanids. In it 'Umar gives a definition of 'justice' that is principally concerned with distribution:

ʿUmar accompanied the troops from Ṣirār to al-Aʿwaṣ. Then he stood up to address them and said: 'God has made for you similitudes and clarified for you the words in order to infuse new life into the hearts, because the hearts are dead in their chests until God revives them. Whoever knows something, let him benefit from it. Justice has its signs {...} and indications {...}, and these signs are diffidence, generosity, and gentleness. The indication of justice is mercy. God has provided for everything a door and for every door a key; the door of justice is reflection, and its key is {asceticism} (*zuhd*). Reflection is remembering death by keeping in mind those who have died and preparing oneself for it by performing the commandments. Piety is taking what is due from everybody who owes it and giving what is due to everybody who has a right to it. Do not grant favor to anyone in this matter. Do not give more than bare livelihood; a person who is not satisfied with this, nothing will make him content. I am between you and God, and nobody is between me and Him. God has obliged me to prevent [your] petitions from reaching Him; bring your complaints therefore to us. Whoever is not able to do this, let him hand the complaint over to someone who can bring it to us; we shall willingly take whatever is due to him on his behalf [and hand it over to him].' (Ibid, 11–12)

Justice was put into practice when 'Umar, after the conquests, distributed the Mesopotamian lands to the Arab commanders. Tabari introduces this narrative with the words:

'During this year 'Umar made a just division between the Kufans and Basrans of the [material benefits of their respective] conquests (*ʿaddala ʿUmaru futūḥa ahl al-Kūfa wa al-Baṣra baynahum*)' (see *History*, xiv/Smith. 43). In a similar vein, Tabari reports on how 'Umar signed contracts with each of the governors of the conquered territories, stipulating the right of the conquered peoples (*ahl al-dhimma*) to their lives, property, law, religion, and the state's obligation to protect the same. For the more distant, formerly Sassanid provinces, Tabari cited in full the treaties signed between each individual governor and the representative of the state. According to Tabari, 'Umar also 'used to require his governors every year to perform the pilgrimage, thereby restraining them from any [act of] tyranny and preventing them from [doing any such thing]' (ibid, 34). As we have seen, the pilgrimage is the ritual celebration of the covenant, and to take part in it on an annual basis would thus remind the governors of their binding obligation towards both the state and its subjects.

'Umar was assassinated by Abu Lu'lu'a, a Christian slave of Persian origins, in the year 644. He had asked 'Umar to reduce the tax on the work he produced as carpenter, but 'Umar had refused to do so since he found the amount reasonable. As he was dying, 'Umar commanded the Companion 'Abd al-Rahman b. 'Awf to gather an electoral council. The council included 'Uthman b. 'Affan of the Banu Abi Mu'ayt branch of the Umayyads and 'Ali b. Abi Talib (the Prophet's cousin and son-in-law) of the Banu Hashim. In a farewell address to them, 'Umar emphasized that the state must remain free of tribal loyalties:

If you should take authority over the people, ʿAlī, I implore you not to bring them under the power of Banū Hāshim. If you should take authority over the people, ʿUthmān, I implore you not to bring them under the power of Banū Abī Muʿayṭ. If you should take authority over the people, Saʿd, I implore you not to bring them under the power of your relatives. Off you go! Consult together, then do what you have to do. (Ibid, 92)

The consultation lasted for three days, during which 'Umar passed away. The outcome was that 'Uthman b. 'Affan was elected caliph.

Tabari's account of 'Uthman's caliphate (644–56) contains some of the finest examples of his technique of juxtaposing reports with different views and explanations, and his attention to psychological detail. His depiction of the build-up to a crisis, and its disastrous solution with 'Uthman's murder, is a literary masterpiece. Tabari divided 'Uthman's caliphate into two periods of six years each. Interestingly, the moderate Zaydi Shi'i view was that during the first six years, up to the point when 'Uthman rejected 'Ali's advice, his rule was legitimate, but not the last six years.[1] In Tabari's narrative, the sixth year (650–51) begins with the conquest of Tabaristan and its 'idolaters' by 'Uthman's commander Sa'id b. al-'As. The conquerors do not come across as heroic or noble; indeed one of the tribal contingents is ridiculed (see *History*, xv/Humphreys. 42–3). The fact that there is only one survivor from a conquered fortress gives the impression that the conquest of Tabaristan was nothing but plunder.

In the second six-year period 'Uthman lost the signet ring of the Prophet. Tabari reports from Ibn 'Abbas that the Prophet had a silver signet ring made for himself, with the inscription, 'Muhammad, the Messenger of God'. He used it to seal his correspondence with foreign rulers, among others the Sassanid king Khusraw Parviz. When the Prophet died, the ring passed to Abu Bakr, then to 'Umar, and finally to 'Uthman. One day in Madina, while sitting at the edge of a well, 'Uthman fiddled with the ring, which slipped from his hand into the well. 'Uthman had the well drained but the ring was not recovered. He had a copy made for himself

[1] See Madelung, 'Imāma'.

which he wore until his death, but that too disappeared thereafter. (Ibid, 62–4)

Before this incident, 'Uthman comes across as well-intentioned but often over-hasty and imprudent, notably in his appointments and dealings with provincial governors and commanders. For example, in Iraq, his appointment and subsequent deposition of his governor al-Walid b. 'Uqba was done in a way that engendered enmity between important Iraqi families; this, as Tabari points out, had consequences for the later war between 'Uthman's nephew Mu'awiya and the caliph 'Ali (ibid, 15–17, 45–62). Likewise, 'Uthman stripped the governor and conqueror of Egypt, 'Amr b. al-'As, of his authority over the land tax and army, giving these positions to 'Abd Allah b. Sa'd, to reward his successful campaigns on the front in Ifriqiyya (Tunisia). Even if the deposition of 'Amr could be justified by his failure to bring in as much tax revenue as he should have, the Caliph's actions provoked enmity. (Ibid, 18–24)

According to Tabari, 'Uthman's crucial mistake, given symbolical expression by his loss of the signet ring, was that in his sixth year as caliph, he changed one of the pilgrimage rites: instead of two prostrations at the station of Mina, where Satan is ritually stoned, as the Prophet, 'Umar and Abu Bakr had done following the precedent of Abraham, 'Uthman suddenly made four. In a report from Ibn 'Abbas, 'Ali asks 'Uthman how he could change the Prophet's *sunna*, and 'Uthman simply says that in his opinion this was a better way to do it. In another report from the Madinan historian al-Waqidi, when asked the same thing, 'Uthman explained that he had done it out of consideration for people from other parts of the caliphate (ibid, 38–9). Given that the pilgrimage is the celebration of God's covenant, 'Uthman's altering, because it suited him, the very part of the ritual where the believers reject Satan is construed as a violation of the covenant itself.

The effects of this come to the fore after the loss of the signet ring: 'Uthman set aside the interests of the state in favour of his kin. For example, he put the whole of Syria under the governorship of his nephew Mu'awiya. This was not wilful nepotism; 'Uthman needed to replace other governors who had become incapacitated. Still, he did not think through the possible consequences of the appointment. Tabari makes it clear that the civil war between Mu'awiya and 'Ali could not have come about if Mu'awiya had not been able to build up a power base in Syria. Thus 'Uthman did not follow the rational policy that 'Umar had pleaded for on his deathbed, namely to resist the temptation to appoint relatives lest the 'tribal forces' of family interest and honour undermine the state. That this is what happened is brought out in a report from the Madinan historian al-Waqidi, where 'Ali is giving 'Uthman his opinion about what had gone wrong:

The people assembled and spoke to ʿAli b. Abī Ṭālib, and he entered ʿUthmān's presence and said, 'The people stand behind me, and they have spoken to me about you. By God, I do not know what to say to you. I know nothing of which you are ignorant, nor can I point out to you any affair with which you are not well acquainted. {…} In no affair have we been assigned greater distinction than you. You have seen and heard the Messenger of God; you were one of his Companions and became a son-in-law to him. (Abū Bakr) b. Abū Quḥāfa was not better suited than you to act rightly, nor did (ʿUmar) b. al-Khaṭṭāb enjoy greater merit in any way, and indeed you had a closer blood-relationship to the Messenger of God [than either of them] {…} nor did they have any precedence over you. Remember God! You are not being given your sight after you were blind, by God, nor are you being instructed after you were in ignorance. Verily the path is manifest and clear, and the signposts of true religion are standing upright. {…} I tell you to beware of God and His sudden assault and His vengeance, for His punishment is harsh and painful indeed. I tell you to beware lest you be the murdered imam of this Community. Indeed it is said that an imam will be killed in this Community, and that bloody strife will be loosed upon it until the Day of

Resurrection, and its affairs will become hopelessly entangled. (God) will leave them as sects (*shiyaᶜ*), and they will not see the truth due to the great height of falsehood. They will toss therein like waves and wander in confusion.' (Ibid, 141–2)

'Ali's address is masterful rhetoric: he is properly humble before the caliph, stressing the latter's merits and proximity to the Prophet; his criticism is voiced through references to God's vengeance, an ominous prophecy about 'the killed imam', and the dreadful consequences of schism and factionalism. Having thus claimed the moral high ground, he proceeds to specific criticisms after 'Uthman's reply:

Then ᶜUthmān replied, 'By God, I knew that (people) would be saying what you have said. But by God, if you were in my place I would not have berated you nor left you in the lurch nor shamed you nor behaved foully. If I have favoured kinsmen, filled a need, sheltered an impoverished wretch, and appointed as governors men like those whom ᶜUmar used to appoint, [then what have I done wrong?]' {…} ᶜAlī said, 'I will tell you that everyone appointed by ᶜUmar b. al-Khaṭṭāb was kept under close scrutiny by him. If (ᶜUmar) heard a single word concerning him he would flog him, then punish him with the utmost severity. But you do not do [that]. You have been weak and easygoing with your relatives.' 'They are your relatives as well,' answered ᶜUthmān. ᶜAlī said, 'By my life, they are closely related to me indeed, but merit is found in others.' ᶜUthmān said, 'Do you know that 'Umar kept Muᶜāwiyah in office throughout his entire caliphate, and I have only done the same.' ᶜAlī answered, 'I adjure you by God, do you know that Muᶜāwiyah was more afraid of ᶜUmar than was ᶜUmar's own slave Yarfa'?' 'Yes,' said (ᶜUthmān). 'Ali went on, 'In fact Muᶜāwiyah makes decisions on issues without [consulting] you, and you know it. Thus, he says to the people{,} "This is ᶜUthmān's command." You hear of this, but do not censure him.' (Ibid, 142–3)

After these words, 'Ali left the assembly. But 'Uthman did not take 'Ali's counsel to his heart. He stuck to his guns and defended his policy:

> By God, you have surely blamed me for things like those which you accepted from Ibn al-Khaṭṭāb. {...} Nay, but which of your rights are you deprived of? By God, I have achieved no less than did my predecessors or those about whose [standing in the Community] you have not disagreed. There is a surplus of wealth, so why should I not do as I wish with the surplus? Why otherwise did I become imām? (Ibid, 143–4)

By his refusal to alter course, 'Uthman sealed the tragic end of his caliphate and life. It illustrates how, according to Tabari's exposition in his Introduction, irrational choices can lead to disastrous outcomes. But never are we told that 'Uthman did not have a choice; in fact, he was given plenty of advice on how to change. He is thus the first example in Islamic history of the king who favours himself more than God, for it was his stubbornness that blinded him to 'Ali's criticism.

This is not to say that Tabari justifies what eventually happened to 'Uthman; on the contrary, his murder is presented as what it was, a terrible crime. In a narrative of almost unbearable psychological detail (ibid, 145–222), Tabari recounts the events which led to the murder of 'Uthman and his family. The narrative is composed of reports from different historians, the most important being the Kufan Sayf b. 'Umar, who portrayed 'Uthman in positive terms, and the Madinan al-Waqidi, who stressed his mistakes. The reports from Sayf b. 'Umar inform us that a revolutionary sect, the Saba'is, with origins in Yemen and branches in Iraq and Egypt, had recruited agents to overthrow 'Uthman's caliphate. These agents made their way to Madina, laid siege to the city, and eventually killed 'Uthman. 'Uthman himself did as well as could be expected in all essential matters against impossible odds (ibid, 149–69). Al-Waqidi reported that, in addition to the siege by the Egyptian conspirators, 'Amr b. al-'As, whom 'Uthman had had deposed as governor of Egypt, tried to get even more people on board the rebellion against 'Uthman (ibid, 170–

72). According to both Sayf b. 'Umar and al-Waqidi, 'Ali, though he was approached by the rebels, never swayed in his loyalty to 'Uthman, in spite of his criticism of his policies. Rather, as al-Waqidi reports, he made a further attempt to guide 'Uthman. (Ibid, 173)

According to a report from Ibn Ishaq, 'Ali and 'Uthman agreed that he would be given a three-day respite to have his governors removed, and address the injustices suffered by the people. 'Ali took 'Uthman's promise to the people, who granted him the respite and promised to accept his repentance after that. 'Ali then put the agreement in writing: '{ʿAlī} bound {ʿUthmān} in this document as tightly as God had ever bound one of His creatures by {contract (*ʿahd*) or covenant (*mīthāq*)}. (ʿAlī) had (the document) witnessed by a body of the leading Emigrants and Helpers' (ibid, 188). However, 'Uthman broke the contract and instead prepared for war, trying to fight his way out of the siege. The besiegers struck back mercilessly and humiliated and killed the caliph and his wife.

In his customary concluding list of 'Uthman's good deeds, Tabari reports on his generosity and good intentions. This, taken together with the reports from Sayf b. 'Umar, which emphasized the Saba'i conspiracy, and those of al-Waqidi, which stressed 'Uthman's mistakes, leave the reader with the impression that 'Uthman was unbalanced – soft when he should have been hard, and stubborn when he should have been flexible – but nonetheless a pious and well-intentioned Muslim; therefore his killers violated the covenant much more intractably than he.

The last of the four Madinan caliphs was 'Ali b. Abi Talib, the Prophet's cousin and son-in-law (*History*, vols. 16–17). Again, Tabari presents us with a harrowing narrative, for which, again, Sayf b. 'Umar is one of the major sources. However, this account is less agonizing in that there is nothing that can be held against 'Ali, who is a much less complicated character than 'Uthman. 'Ali comes across as the paragon of virtue, with the possible weakness of pride in his own good judgement and morals.

According to reports from Sayf b. 'Umar, after the Egyptian besiegers had murdered 'Uthman, they promised to respect the people of Madina in their choice of caliph. When the people elected 'Ali and swore allegiance, the besiegers dispersed and Madina's authority was almost but not entirely restored, in that, as Tabari remarks, 'the outsiders and riffraff came to have a say in it', by which he meant the Saba'i besiegers (*History*, xvi/Brockett. 15). Problems arose as soon as 'Ali appointed governors and dispatched them to their provinces. In Egypt, his appointee, Qays b. Sa'd, was accepted by about a third of the leading Egyptian officials, but resisted by the others; the same happened in Basra. In Yemen and Kufa, however, 'Ali and his governors were accepted. The greatest problem was Syria under 'Uthman's powerful nephew Mu'awiya. 'Ali's governor, Sahl b. Hunayf, was turned back to Madina by Mu'awiya's scouts as soon as he set foot on Syrian territory. Whenever 'Ali sought allegiance from Mu'awiya, the only responses he got were threats that Mu'awiya held him responsible for the murder of 'Uthman. Eventually, 'Ali decided to consider these threats a declaration of war, and prepared to march on Syria. At this point, he got news that a contingent from Makka, comprising Abu Bakr's relatives Talha and al-Zubayr, and his daughter 'A'isha, the Prophet's favourite wife, had made common cause with Mu'awiya and set out for Basra, to stage a revolt against him on charges that he had been involved in the murder of 'Uthman.

This was the build-up to the famous Battle of the Camel (December 656), named after the red camel ridden by 'A'isha. 'Ali's supporters and fighters were from Madina and Kufa, while his enemies were based in Makka, Basra and Syria. 'Ali was victorious, but at an enormous cost:

From Sayf (b. ʿUmar): Those killed at the Battle of the Camel around the camel numbered 10,000, half from ʿAlī's followers and half from ʿĀʾishah's. Two thousand Azdīs fell plus 500 from the rest of al-Yaman. Two thousand from Muḍar fell plus 500 from Qays, 500 from Tamīm, 1,000 from Banū Dabbah, and 500 from Bakr b. Wāʾil.

It was said that in the first battle, 5,000 Baṣrans were killed and a further 5,000 in the second battle, totalling 10,000 Baṣran fatalites and 5,000 Kūfans.

Seventy elders of Banū ʿAdī were killed that day, all of whom were well versed in the Qurʾān. Youths and men who were not so well versed in the Qurʾān were also killed. ʿĀʾishah said, 'I was still hoping for victory until I heard the voices of Banū ʿAdī subside.' (Ibid, 164)

Another report estimated fatalities at some 6000 (ibid, 171). The political and moral consequences were equally disastrous. After the event, the battle has been referred to as 'the first *fitna*,' or 'first infighting.' The battle seemed to confirm 'Ali in his authority as caliph; he pardoned 'A'isha and every surviving fighter, because he did not want to continue the killing:

It was part of ʿAlī's practice not to kill those who fled or to finish off the wounded or to dishonor women, or to take money. So on that day some men asked, 'What allows us to kill them but forbids us their money?' 'Those who fought you are like you,' ʿAlī replied. 'Those who make peace with us are one with us, and we are one with them, but, for those who persist until they get struck by us, I fight them to the death. You are in no need of their fifth.' It was on that day the Khawārij began talking among themselves. (Ibid, 166–67)

'The Khawārij' refers to a group who initially supported 'Ali, but turned against him because of his readiness to compromise and negotiate with enemies. Literally, *khawārij* (sing. *khārijī*) means 'those who have gone outside,' and refers to subsequent developments when this group withdrew from the community of Muslims and claimed for themselves the right to declare other Muslims, whose deeds did not meet their approval, as apostates. In theological terms, they held that faith consisted in deeds, not belief, and that the most important deed was *jihad*. Hence, the caliph had to be the most pious of men, and wage *jihad*.

Since the first civil war had been proven insufficient to wrest the caliphate from ʻAli, Muʻawiya plotted a second. He planted false intelligence about ʻAli's governors, so that a vicious circle of suspicion and misguided counter-measures would undermine ʻAli's power from within. This is an issue that clearly divides Tabari and the Hanbalis: the latter were entirely on the side of Muʻawiya as champion of the murdered ʻUthman against ʻAli, while Tabari's narratives are evidently in ʻAli's favour.

When ʻAli eventually found out about Muʻawiya's plotting, he decided to confront him. This led to the Battle of Siffin, on the Syrian Euphrates plain in 657. Volume 17 of the English translation of the *History* is devoted to this battle and its aftermath, ending with the murder of ʻAli by a Khariji in 661. Before the battle, ʻAli appointed his cousin Ibn ʻAbbas (see above, p. 27) as governor of Basra. He himself moved to Kufa, where he prepared to command his army in person.

Abu Mikhnaf, a historian from Kufa who is the main source for Tabari's narratives about ʻAli and his descendants, reports that Muʻawiya's forces set up camp so as to block ʻAli's troops from the Euphrates, in order to weaken them by thirst after their march north from Kufa. In the first round of the battle, however, ʻAli beat back Muʻawiya's forces and made a way to the water, so that his troops could drink and fill their waterskins. With his characteristic compassion, he also let Muʻawiya's men drink.

The battle went on for months at low intensity, and then the parties agreed to a truce during the sacred month al-Muharram. During the truce, Tabari reports from Abu Mikhnaf, that Muʻawiya sent messengers asking ʻAli to renounce his caliphate because of his involvement in the murder of ʿUthman. ʿAli's reported response sets out what would be the later Imami Shiʿi position on the legitimacy of the first three caliphs, and the special status of the family of the Prophet, i.e., ʿAli, Fatima, and their sons:

God sent Muḥammad with the truth and through him provided deliverance from error, salvation from destruction, and the overcoming of division. Then God took him to Himself after he had carried out his mission. The people appointed Abū Bakr as caliph, and Abū Bakr appointed ʿUmar after him, and those two conducted themselves well and led the community with justice. We resented their ruling over us, the family of the Messenger of God, but we excused them for that. Then ʿUthmān ruled and did things that the people found reprehensible, so that they came to him and killed him. Afterward they came to me, who was keeping out of their concerns, and they asked me to accept the oath of allegiance. I refused, but they insisted and said that the community would never find anyone acceptable but me and that, if I did not, they were afraid that division would result. So I accepted the oath of allegiance from them. But then I was surprised to find the dissension of two of those who had given me the oath of allegiance and the opposition of Muʿāwiyah, to whom God had given neither precedence in accepting the religion nor forebears of good character in Islam. He is one of those who were set free (*ṭalīq*) by the Prophet, and the son of one of them, a member of those 'parties' that persisted in enmity to God, His Prophet, and the Muslims, both he and his father, until they reluctantly entered Islam. But it is a surprise that you take part in his opposition and are led by him, abandoning the family of your Prophet, against which you must not show discord and opposition nor place any one on the same level. I call you to God's {*written document* (*kitāb Allāh*)}, the precedent (*sunnah*) of His Prophet, the suppression of what is false, and putting into practice the signs of the religion. That is what I have to say, and I ask God's pardon for me and for you and for every Believer, male and female, and every Muslim, male and female. (*History*, xvii/Hawting. 25–6)

After this speech, the messengers demanded of 'Ali that he testify that 'Uthman was killed unjustly. But 'Ali replied starkly: 'I will not say either that he was killed unjustly or that his killing was justified, because he was unjust himself' (ibid, 26). As Mu'awiya refused to withdraw, fighting was resumed shortly after, on 'Ali's initiative. When 'Ali's Iraqi forces were gaining the upper hand, Tabari reports, Mu'awiya's chief commander came up with a psychological trick: his men raised amulets containing Qur'anic writing on their spearheads and called the people back to the unity of 'God's written document' (*kitāb Allāh*), implying that 'Ali's men were breaking up the community. 'Ali, according to Tabari's source, Abu Mikhnaf, saw through the trick:

ᶜAlī said: 'Servants of God, carry on fighting your enemies, for you have truth and right on your side. Muᶜāwiyah, ᶜAmr b. al-ᶜĀṣ, Ibn Abī Muᶜayṭ, Ḥabīb b. Maslamah, Ibn Abī Sarḥ, and al-Ḍaḥḥak b. Qays are men without religion and without Qurʾān. I know them better than you, for I was with them both as children and as men, and they were the worst of children and the worst of men. Alas for you! {…} They have raised {the *maṣāḥif*} up to you only to deceive you, to outwit you, and to trick you.' They answered him, 'If we are called to God's {*written document*},[1] we are bound to respond.' ᶜAlī said to them, 'The only reason I have fought against them was so that they should adhere to the authority of this {*written document*},[1] for they have disobeyed God in what He has commanded and they have forgotten His {contract (*ᶜahdahu*)} and rejected His {*written document*}.' (Ibid, 79)

'Ali's argument was opposed by a man who had taken part in the murder of 'Uthman, and who would later join the Kharijis against 'Ali:

Misᶜar b. Fadakī al-Tamīmī and Zayd b. Ḥusayn al-Ṭāʾī, al-Sinbisī, who were with a band of the [Qur'an readers] who later became Khawārij, said to him: ' ᶜAlī, respond to the {*written document*} of

---

[1] I have here, as before, replaced 'God's Book' (*kitāb Allāh*) with 'God's written document'.

God when you are called to it. Otherwise we shall indeed deliver you up entirely to the enemy or do what we did with [ʿUthmān] Ibn ʿAffān. It is our duty to act in accordance with what is in {God's *written document*}. We have accepted it and, by God, if you do not do what we tell you, we will do what we say.' ʿAlī said, 'Do not forget that I forbade you to do this, and remember your words to me. As for me, if you are obedient to me, fight, and, if disobedient, then do whatever seems best to you.' (Ibid)

The trick having succeeded in breaking the unity of 'Ali's forces, he was forced to accept arbitration, i.e., to settle the conflict through two mediators, and signed a contract with Mu'awiya to do this. He thereby implicitly conceded that his right to the caliphate was open to negotiation. According to Abu Mikhnaf, the hypocrisy of the Kharijis now became evident, as they turned against him for refusing to fight for his right to the caliphate! (ibid, 100–4, 111–41). Tabari makes it clear that 'Ali consistently held to the obligations of the covenant, namely to abide by written agreements, while the Khariji, Hurqus, tried to make him break it:

According to Abū Mikhnāf: {…} Ḥurqūs said to [ʿAlī], 'Repent of your sin, retract your decision, and come out with us against our enemies whom we will fight until we meet our Lord.' ʿAlī answered them, 'That is what I wanted you to do, but you disobeyed me and now we have a written agreement with them and stipulated conditions, and we have made them promises and given them our word concerning it. God has said, "Observe God's {contract (*ʿahd*)} when you have entered into it and do not break your oaths after you have pledged them, for now you have made God your guarantor. God knows what you do." ' Ḥurqūs said, 'That is a sin (*dhanb*) from which you must repent,' but ʿAlī answered, 'It is no sin but only a failure of judgement (*raʾy*) and weakness of action. I enjoined you concerning it and told you not to do it.' (Ibid, 111)

Abu Mikhnaf's report pinpoints what 'Ali's mistake was, namely his signing the contract which now bound him. However, there was not much he could have done, after the Kharijis had split his ranks, to avoid doing that.

'Ali spent the last two years of his caliphate fighting on two fronts. He battled the Kharijis, who terrorized ordinary people with extraordinary cruelty. 'Ali is quoted as pointing out the hypocrisy underpinning their dogma of faith by deeds, which gave them licence to kill those whom they did not count as Muslims: 'By God, if you killed even a chicken like that, its killing would be a weighty matter with God. How will it be, then, regarding a soul the killing of which God has prohibited?' (ibid, 130). 'Ali eventually crushed the Kharijis, although their ideology and supporters lived on.

The other front was with Mu'awiya, who had now seized Egypt, an important source of tax revenue for 'Ali. In May 660, Mu'awiya sent troops into 'Ali's remaining territory: Iraq, Persia, and, finally, the Hijaz itself. A year later, in May 661, three members of the Kharijis conspired to each kill one of the three men of authority in the Islamic domain, 'Ali, Mu'awiya, and 'Amr b. al-'As, so that their movement could seize power. One Ibn Muljam took upon himself to kill 'Ali. With the help of other Kharijis in Kufa, he attacked 'Ali as he came out unarmed from the mosque. 'Ali died of his wounds. Mu'awiya and 'Amr b. al-'As survived the attempts to murder them, and instead had their assailants killed. 'Ali's eldest son al-Hasan, after he had said his farewell to his father, killed Ibn Muljam.

'Ali's caliphate fits the pattern, explained in Tabari's Introduction, of kings who govern rationally and follow God's guidance but are defeated in this world, and whose reward is stored up in the hereafter. 'Ali held to his right as elected caliph but the odds were against him, once Mu'awiya became determined to seize the caliphate for himself. If there is one thing 'Ali could have done differently, it was to concede that 'Uthman had been unjustly murdered; his statement that 'Uthman was unjust made it easy for Mu'awiya to insist on 'Ali's complicity. Pride may have been what prevented 'Ali from making that concession: he knew the truth and would speak it, regardless of the consequences.

THE DYNASTIC CALIPHATES

Mu'awiya's caliphate (661–80) is significant because succession thereafter was dynastic. As Tabari pointed out in *Sarih al-sunna*, caliphate was thereby effectively kingship. Mu'awiya was of the Banu Sufyan, a branch of the Umayyad family of Quraysh which ruled from 661 to 683. With his accession, the seat of power was transferred from Madina to Damascus. New conquests were made, especially in North Africa against the Byzantines. The principle of dynastic succession was established when, in the year 675 or 6, Mu'awiya made his son Yazid heir apparent. After Yazid's rule (680–83; *History*, vol. 19) another branch of the Umayyad family took over, the Banu Marwan (vols. 20–27). The caliphate remained in their hands through dynastic succession until 749, when the Banu 'Abbas of the Prophet's family Banu Hashim took power through a *coup d'état*. Their seizure of power also involved a regional shift of the power centre, this time from Syria and Damascus to Mesopotamia and the new 'Abbasid capital Baghdad, founded in 762.

The Madina caliphate was in some respects closer to the tribal model than the dynastic caliphates, for just as the shaykh 'emerged' within a family through consultative processes leading to consensus, so the first four caliphs were elected from the Quraysh through consultation. But it also mirrored Plato's political theory, that merit must be the principle governing appointments of state functionaries at all levels. This principle of *personal*, as opposed to family-based, merit allowed 'Uthman to be elected, in spite of his family's appalling record as the Prophet's fiercest opponents. And although 'Uthman favoured his relatives in the nepotistic or 'tribal' sense, it was in fact 'Ali who first introduced the idea of succession from father to son when he appointed his son al-

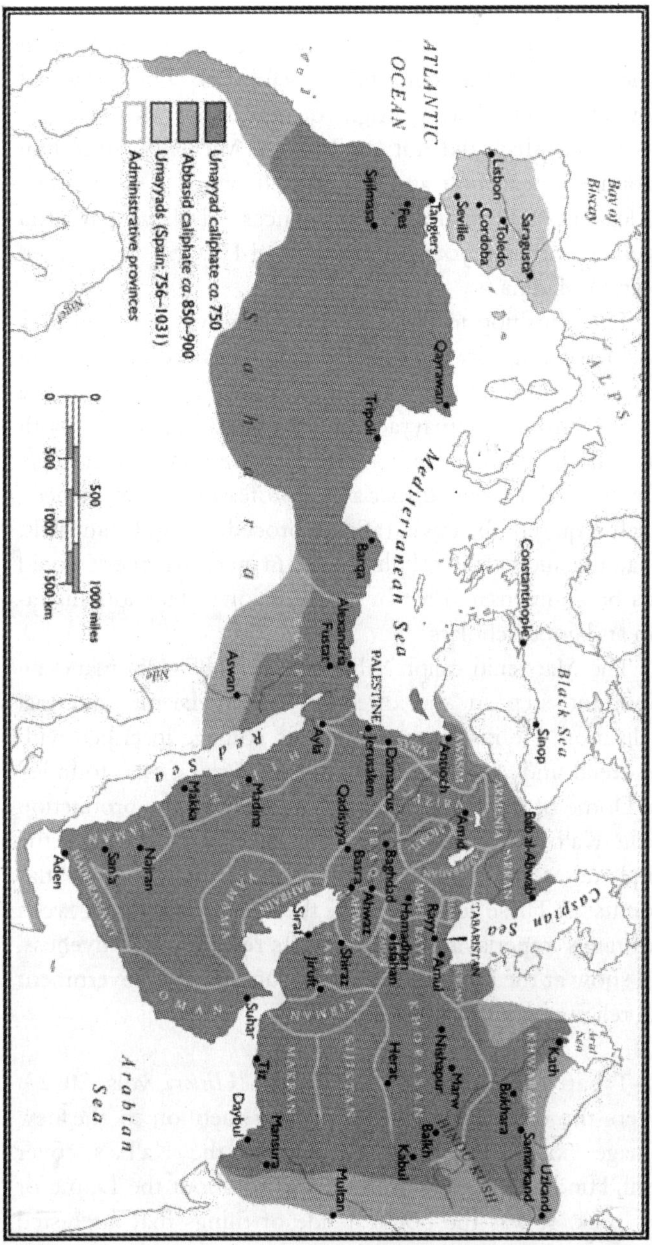

Map 6. *The Umayyad and 'Abbasid caliphates at the peak of their power*

Hasan as successor. For ʿAli and the later ʿAlids, merit coincided with the dynastic principle, so that only the Prophet's family had the right qualifications. However, al-Hasan's caliphate did not last because Muʿawiya made him renounce it peacefully and was himself sworn in as caliph by the leaders of all the imperial provinces. Al-Hasan left Kufa together with his younger brother, al-Husayn, and settled down in Madina.

The transition to dynastic succession was matched by a division of authority between the caliph as head of state, and those dedicated to the religion, eventually *al-ʿulamāʾ*, 'the scholars'. In the Umayyad and ʿAbbasid caliphates, both state affairs and religious sciences became increasingly complex and demanded specialized professional competences, which required objective, rational procedures and standards. What the individual caliph lacked in personal merit could thus be compensated for by a professional state administration and good scholars.

The Marwanid caliph ʿAbd al-Malik (685–705) marks an important step in the direction of an Islamic imperial civilization. He instituted an Islamic coinage inscribed with the creed and Arabic as the imperial *lingua franca*, founded the Dome of the Rock in Jerusalem, ordered the production of the Kaʿba's brocade cover, and significantly extended the caliphate's territories in North Africa, as far as the Atlas Mountains. These activities show the interconnection between the state's imperial ambitions and its religious assertiveness, and show at the same time that the functions of government and religion were clearly separated.

Tabari's account of ʿAbd al-Malik (*History*, vols. 20–23) covers the conquests, gives a passing mention to the new coinage (xxii/Rowson. 90ff.), and to the Kaʿba's cover (xxiii/Hinds. 181), and has not a word about the Dome of the Rock. It was the political side of things that interested

Tabari as historian, i.e. the conquests and the internal political problems, rather than the propagandistic side of religion. The same pattern is noticeable in the remaining narratives about Umayyad and 'Abbasid history: he focuses on succession, the appointments of governors and viziers, conquests, administration, and rebellions and their causes (including taxation practices). In the following section, we shall see how he presented these matters, from the viewpoint of relations between the 'Alids and the state.

THE 'ALIDS AND THE STATE

In the dynastic caliphates the caliph was legitimized in religious terms but was not theocratic in the sense of 'both king and priest'. The situation was different with the 'Alid *Imam*s, i.e. the descendants of 'Ali b. Abi Talib. They perceived themselves to be the rightful heirs to the caliphate, because they were the closest kin to the Prophet, and combined in their persons both political and spiritual authority. From the viewpoint of the ruling dynasties, the 'Alids therefore constituted a kind of royalty, with specific rights to allowances from the state, but which could never be allowed to rule.

Tabari distinguished firmly between the Shi'a and the 'Alids. In his view, the problem of Shi'i anti-state movements had already begun during 'Uthman's caliphate (644–56), when the Saba'i movement emerged in Yemen and spread to the Hijaz, Iraq and Egypt. He did not object to the historian Sayf b. 'Umar's information that members of this movement were behind the murder of 'Uthman, and that the Kharijis, who first emerged during the conflict between 'Ali and Mu'awiya, were a continuation of the Saba'i movement. However, neither the Saba'is nor the Kharijis had anything to do with the 'Alid appeal to kinship with the

Prophet. To the contrary, the Kharijis rejected, to the most extreme degree, the dynastic principle in favour of 'merit'.

The ninth-century Shi'i anti-state movements (the Zanj movement, the Qarmatians, and the Fatimids) were different: these all based their claims to power on kinship with the Prophet through 'Ali and Fatima. However, Tabari did not recognize their genealogies as valid. On the Zanj movement, Tabari wrote that it began in the Basra region in 870 with a man who 'claimed' that his name was 'Ali b. Muhammad b. Ahmad b. 'Ali b. 'Isa b. Zayd b. 'Ali b. al-Husayn b. 'Ali, for whom his sources reported another lineage to the tribe 'Abd al-Qays. Tabari had noted that during the 'apostasy wars' under Abu Bakr, 'Abd al-Qays in eastern Arabia had briefly proclaimed as their ruler a Christian of the Banu Lakhm, the former Sassanid vassals (*History*, x/Donner. 134–7). Tabari thus implied that 'Ali b. Muhammad had fabricated the 'Alid genealogy in order to gain followers (*History*, xxxvi/Waines. 31).

Tabari's main source on the Zanj rebellion was Muhammad b. Sahl, originally part of the rebellion, who in his turn referred to three other sources, also from within the movement. Taken together, the reports present a balanced view of what motivated the rebellion, of its individual supporters, and its destructive effects as seen both from within and from an 'Abbasid point of view. As Hugh Kennedy has remarked, the 'insiders' of the rebellion claim to be Muslims, while the 'Abbasid 'outsiders' call them 'enemies of Islam' and declare jihad against them.[1] Tabari seems to agree with the 'Abbasid view, at least judging from his earlier comment about 'Abd al-Qays' Christian roots and preferences.

'Ali b. Muhammad instigated a revolt among the so-called Zanj, slave labourers of African origin, whose main task it was to remove the nitrous topsoil of the marshlands

---

1 Hugh Kennedy (2003), 'Caliphs and their Chroniclers', 17–35.

in the Mesopotamian delta. Their work was vitally important for the 'Abbasid state as the lands could not otherwise be used for agriculture. 'Ali b. Muhammad convinced the Zanj that he was the returned Messiah, or al-Mahdi, 'the divinely guided one', and that his just rule would liberate them from their oppressors, the 'Abbasid governors. He had also travelled around the central caliphate gathering supporters for his cause, with Bahrayn as a stronghold. Like the Kharijis, this movement was brutally violent, in spite of its promises of justice: beheadings of the enemy were a speciality, and looting and killing of the peasants (ibid, 47–9, 66–8) It took until 883 before the movement was finally defeated.

The Qarmatian movement began in the Sawad outside Kufa in the year 891–92, with the arrival there of a man from the province of Khuzistan, in western Iran. The man was called Qarmat (hence 'the Qarmatian movement'), Tabari explained, because he took up residence with an Aramaic-speaking peasant called 'Karmita', 'the red-eyed one'; in Arabic, it was pronounced as 'Qarmat' (*History*, xxxvii/Fields. 171). Tabari's source about the Qarmatians is the scribe Muhammad b. Dawud b. al-Jarrah, of the family of 'Ali b. 'Isa, who had questioned one of the movement's leaders after their defeat. According to his reports, Qarmat had contacted the Zanj leader before the latter's death in 883, declaring that he subscribed to a specific religious practice and that he was prepared to offer his men in support of the Zanj; but this came to nothing as they had disagreed on essential matters (ibid, 175). Qarmat thus went ahead on his own, and founded what Tabari's source called a 'new religion':

Settling in a place known as al-Nahrayn, he led an ascetic life and displayed his piety to all. He earned his living by weaving baskets from palm leaves, and spent much of his time praying. He continued this way for some time. If anyone joined him, he would discourse with him upon religious affairs, inculcate him with contempt for this world, and teach him that it was incumbent upon everyone to pray fifty times each day and night. He did this until news spread about his activity in this place. Then he disclosed that he was urging allegiance to an Imām from the house of the Messenger. He went on in this manner attracting people to his side and spreading his message which won over their hearts. (Ibid, 169–70)

Tabari's source made a connection between Qarmat's religion and Christianity, reporting that Qarmat 'selected twelve agents from among them, and he instructed them to summon people to their faith. He said to the agents: "You are like the apostles of Jesus, the son of Mary" ' (ibid, 171). Tabari also reported on other interesting aspects of Qarmat's religious message: it was markedly esoteric, or founded on the assumption that reality has a hidden and secret dimension, which is the Real reality, as opposed to the exoteric, perceptible and misleading reality. In political terms, this translated to mean that the existing 'Abbasid state is false and misleading, whereas the imperceptible, 'hidden' *Imam* is the truth. Since truth is not materially perceptible, it must be gained from discourse, according to the idealist epistemology; the Greek word for 'discourse' is *logos* and in Arabic it is *kalima*. This is yet another reference to Christianity, for in *John* 1. 1–18, 'the Logos' (Arabic *al-kalima*) is the term for Christ. According to Tabari's reports, the Qarmatians introduced a wholly new religion, with Monday as the day of congregation instead of Friday, and a new version of *al-Fatiha*, the opening *sura* of the Qur'an:

Praise God for His Logos {*bi-kalimatihi*}. May He be exalted in His name, bestowed upon His saints through His saints. Say, 'The new moons were given to the people.' Their exoteric meaning allows people to calculate the years and months and days, but the esoteric meaning indicates that they are My Saints, who have taught My worshipers My path. Beware of me, O people of superior mind. I am the one who would not be called to account for his deeds. I am the knowing, I am the wise, and I am the one who will test my worshipers and try my creatures. He who bears patiently my test, trial and experience, I shall place in Paradise, and I will grant him my everlasting grace. But he who deserts my cause and speaks against my messengers will be flung into eternal pain and humiliation. I shall fulfil my purpose and reveal my cause through the tongues of my apostles. I am the one who is not surpassed by any powerful one, but I depose him; nor by any glorious one, but I render him contemptible. But I am not one of those who persist in their ignorance and say, 'I shall continue to cleave to it, and believe it.' For those are the unbelievers. (Ibid, 174)

A very earthly concern underlies the esotericism: tax. 'The new moons' refers to the new dates for tax collection, as opposed to the state governor's dates, and Qarmat did indeed collect a dinar per year from each of his followers (ibid, 171, 173). By thus recruiting the peasant population of the Sawad to his cause, he diverted tax income from the 'Abbasid governors and the state treasury. The authorities in Baghdad were apparently clear about the connection between the religious messages and the subversive movements; Tabari reported that the authorities had decreed that 'no popular preachers, astrologers, or fortune-tellers should sit (and practice their trade) in the streets or in the Friday mosque. Moreover, the book sellers were sworn not to trade in books of theology, polemics or philosophy' (ibid, 176). Between the years 900 and 907, the Qarmatians' war caused the state as well as private persons considerable loss of life, property, and income, including booty from pilgrimage caravans bound for Makka.

Thus Tabari perceived the calls for justice made by these Isma'ili Shi'i leaders as a cover for personal ambition and greed, and as capitalizing on the grievances of certain groups, e.g. the Zanj slave labourers. This is in marked contrast to his reports on the 'Alids, who sought to protect their rights when they were violated. The next 'Alid 'crisis' after the murder of 'Ali was when Mu'awiya swore in his son Yazid as heir to the caliphate. Before doing so, he had made ‘Ali’s eldest son al-Hasan renounce his claims, but the younger son, al-Husayn, had not explicitly done so, and Mu‘awiya died before having obtained his allegiance. Therefore, one of the first things Yazid had to do on becoming caliph was to ensure al-Husayn’s allegiance. Al-Husayn refused, which set in motion a chain of events ending in al-Husayn and his family being killed by Yazid’s governor of Basra, Ibn Ziyad.

Tabari gives two different accounts of these events, the main one on the authority of Abu Mikhnaf, the specialist on the ‘Alids, which will be recapitulated here (*History*, xix/Howard. 22–179). Yazid was effectively caliph over all the provinces, and had appointed his governors. However, al-Husayn in Madina and Abu Bakr’s relative Ibn al-Zubayr in Makka refused to swear allegiance to him. Al-Husayn was advised by his friends to go to Makka, because the people there would support him in any decision he might make. He did so, but realized that Ibn al-Zubayr, who was the leader there, was uncomfortable with his presence because he was effectively his rival. Meanwhile, people in Kufa, his father ‘Ali’s last stronghold, sent messages to al-Husayn saying that they suffered under Yazid’s governor and would join him if he chose to stand up for his right to the caliphate. Al-Husayn’s cousin, Ibn ‘Abbas, heard of this and warned him, reminding him of how his father ‘Ali had been let down by the Kufans at the very moment when he was gaining an upper hand in the battle against Mu‘awiya, and urged him to stay put in Makka. Al-Husayn thanked him for his sincere advice but indicated that he would not follow it. Instead, he decided that God had commanded him to go to Kufa and fight for the caliphate. There, the Kufans did indeed desert him. Before departing for the battle, al-Husayn addressed them, offering them a last chance to repent and join him, stressing the binding nature of contracts and oaths of allegiance:

Al-Ḥusayn preached to his followers and the followers of al-Ḥurr at al-Bīḍah. After praising and glorifying God, {h}e said: 'People, the Apostle of God said, "When anyone sees the authorities make permissible what God has forbidden, violating God's {contract (*ʿahd*)} and opposing the Sunnah of the Apostle of God by acting against the servants of God sinfully and with hostility, when anyone sees all these incidents and does not upbraid them by deed or by word, it is God's decree to make that person subject to fortune." Indeed, these authorities have cleaved to obedience to Satan and have abandoned obedience to the Merciful; they have made corruption visible; they have neglected the punishment (*ḥudūd*) laid down by God; they have appropriated the *fayʾ* [taxes] exclusively to themselves; they have permitted what God has forbidden, and they have forbidden what He has permitted. I have the right to change more than anyone else. Your letters were brought to me, and your messengers came to me with your oath of allegiance that you would not hand me over or desert me. If you fulfil your pledge, you will arrive at true guidance, for I am al-Ḥusayn b. ʿAlī, the son of Fāṭimah, daughter of the Apostle of God. My life is with your lives, my family is with your families. In me you have an ideal model (*uswah*). However, if you will not act, but you break your contract and renounce your responsibility for the oath of allegiance that you have given, then, by my life, it is not a thing that is unknown of you. You have done that to my father, my brother, and my cousin, Muslim. Anyone who was deceived by you would be gullible. Thus have you mistaken your fortune and lost your destiny. For whoever violates his word only violates his own soul. God will enable me to do without you. Peace be with you and the mercy and blessings of God.' (Ibid, 95–6)

The Kufans did not change their minds; al-Husayn set off with his family, including women and children, and a band of seventy-two men: his fighters. The two factions met by the Euphrates, at a place called Karbala, in the year 681. Just as his father 'Ali had been cut off from the river by Mu'awiya's troops, Yazid's commander Ibn Ziyad cut al-Husayn and his men off from the river water, so that they would be weakened by thirst. After heroic fighting, in which al-Husayn and his men exhibited bravery and compassion in equal measure, Ibn Ziyad's men had al-Husayn surrounded.

In a desperate move, al-Husayn spurred on his horse, trying to break through to the river and the life-giving water:

According to Hishām (b. Muḥammad al-Kalbī) – his father, Muḥammad b. al-Sā'ib – al-Qāsim b. al-Aṣbagh b. Nubātah – one of those who was a witness in the camp of al-Ḥusayn: When Ḥusayn's camp was overrun, he rode toward the dam, trying to reach the Euphrates. One of the Banū Abān b. Dārim shouted, 'Woe upon you! Prevent him from getting to the water. Don't let his Shīʿah get to him.' He whipped his horse, and the people followed him so that they prevented al-Ḥusayn from getting to the Euphrates. Then al-Ḥusayn cried out, 'O God! Make him thirsty!' The Abānī took out an arrow and lodged it in al-Ḥusayn's throat. Al-Ḥusayn pulled out the arrow and held out the palms of his hands. Both were filled with blood. Then al-Ḥusayn said, 'O God! I complain to you about what is being done to the son of the daughter of your Prophet.' (Ibid, 156–7)

In the end, al-Husayn was surrounded on all sides, defenceless. But his attackers held back, none wanting to be the one who killed the Prophet's grandson. Finally, one of them called the others forward, and al-Husayn was killed and decapitated. Abu Mikhnaf reported that his body had received thirty-three stab wounds and thirty-four sword blows; others reported that his belongings and clothes were plundered and divided among his killers.

As with Tabari's accounts of the murders of 'Uthman and 'Ali, the reader is left with mixed feelings about the killing of al-Husayn. It represents a significant further step on a downward political slope: first a Companion caliph was killed ('Uthman), then the Prophet's cousin 'Ali, and now the Prophet's grandson. Like his father 'Ali, al-Husayn was idealistic in holding on to principles, and compassionate. But he made irrational choices. Tabari reports that he was given ample warnings about the consequences of responding to the Kufans' siren song. Even though, because of the potential rivalry with Ibn al-Zubayr, it was not uncomplicated for him to remain in Makka, he could have saved his own and his family's lives by staying put and easing Ibn al-Zubayr's discomfiture. That would have been the rational choice, given that the killing of the Prophet's family was a sacrilege in itself, irrespective of the question of who was to be caliph. Tabari ended the narrative by counting all the members of Banu Hashim who were killed at Karbala, and citing two poems which give an idea of how he viewed the killing of al-Husayn. One was recited by Ibn al-Hurr, a Kufan noble who did not manage to help al-Husayn, but afterwards made his way to the battleground, struggling with crippling feelings of guilt, and lamenting:

A treacherous governor, the very reality of a treacherous man, says:
Should you not have fought against the martyr son of Fāṭimah?
O how much I regret that I did not help him!
Indeed, every soul that does not set upon the right course regrets.
Indeed, because I was not among his defenders,
I have a grief that will never depart.
May God constantly water with rain the souls of those who girt themselves to help him.
I stood at their graves and their field of death.
My heart almost burst, and my eyes shed tears.
By my life! They were active in battle, quick to war, noble defenders.
They helped to support the son of the daughter of their Prophet,
like lions from a covert, with their swords.
If they were killed, then every pious soul
on the earth has become downcast in grief for that.
Never have men been seen nobler than they
in the face of death, bright-faced generous lords.
Do you kill them unjustly and hope for our affection?
Leave a course of action that is not suitable for us.
By my life! You have antagonized us by killing them.
How many men and women of us detest you!
Many times I intended to go with many supporters
against an oppressive group who had deviated from the truth.
[…] (Ibid, 182–83)

The poem illustrates well the emotions expressed in the Shi'i passion play (*taʿziya*) that has, since mid-tenth century, been performed annually in Muharram, as a penitentiary rite for all those, past and present, who failed to come to al-Husayn's rescue at Karbala. In the ritual, scenes from the narrative which Tabari reports from Abu Mikhnaf are performed by actors, and accompanied by processions of flagellants. This annual re-enactment of al-Husayn's martyrdom is a Shi'i complement to the common Islamic annual celebration of the covenant in the pilgrimage to the Ka'ba, and signifies that the covenant has been violated and will remain so until an 'Alid *Imam* leads the community.

After the killing of al-Husayn, the remaining members of the family accepted Yazid's caliphate in practice, although in principle they never considered it legitimate. There were numerous 'Alid rebellions against the state, both under Umayyad and 'Abbasid rule, and Kufa remained one of their strongholds, in spite of its people having let down both 'Ali and al-Husayn. However, judging by Tabari's account, these were motivated not by ideology but by mismanagement on the part of the state administration and governors.

This is illustrated in Tabari's narrative of the rebellion of al-Husayn's grandson, Zayd b. 'Ali b. al-Husayn (d. 740), in the reign of the Marwanid caliph, Hisham b. 'Abd al-Malik (723–43). Zayd was a very different character from both 'Ali and al-Husayn – gregarious and, as we saw in Part 1 (above, p. 8), with a taste for women. Even so, according to the narrative (again mainly from Abu Mikhnaf), his revolt developed similarly to al-Husayn's: he was living in Madina, moved to Kufa, and was tempted into rebellion against the state by Kufans who later deserted him (*History*, xxvi/Hillenbrand, 3–55). The causes are presented differently in different reports. According to Abu Mikhnaf, Zayd was involved in litigation between members of the family descended from 'Ali's son al-Hasan and those descended from al-Husayn, each claiming rights to the Prophet's family trust from war booty. At the same time, Zayd became entangled with the caliph's new governor in Iraq, Yusuf b. 'Umar, on another money matter. Yusuf b. 'Umar's predecessor made a claim before him that he had paid Zayd a sum for land in Madina which he had subsequently returned, but that Zayd had not repaid the money. Yusuf b. 'Umar reported this to the caliph, who ordered Zayd to go to Yusuf in order to confront the former governor in Kufa. Zayd did so, the former governor could not prove that any money had changed hands, and Zayd was cleared of all charges (ibid, 5–7). According to other reports, relations between Zayd, the caliph and his governor were tense because Zayd had brought his suit to the caliph, who had insulted him by accusing him of plotting rebellion. (Ibid, 10–13)

Abu Mikhnaf's report says that Zayd stayed on in Kufa after these controversies, and that some Kufans then urged him to take up the 'Alid cause against the Umayyads. Subsequent reports indicate that Zayd took up the cause because of the injustice done to him in the course of the litigation and testimonies. When the Kufans swore the oath of allegiance, he gave the following address in which he mentions both 'pensions' and 'booty', which he felt he had been deprived of:

{According to Abu Mikhnaf: ...} 'We summon you to God's written document and the *sunnah* of His Prophet, and to wage war against those who act tyrannically, to defend those who have been oppressed, to give pensions to those who have been deprived of them, to distribute this booty (*fay'*) equally amongst those who are entitled to it, to make restitution to those who have been wronged, to bring home those who have been detained on the frontiers, and to help the *ahl al-bayt* [{the} Prophet's family] against those who have opposed us and disregard our just cause. Do you swear allegiance on that basis?' If they said, 'Yes,' Zayd would place his hand on theirs and he would say, 'The pledge, treaty, and covenant of God and the {contract (*'ahd*)} of His Prophet are upon you so that you keep your allegiance to me, fight my enemy, and act in good faith toward me both secretly and publicly.' (Ibid, 23)

Zayd's rebellion, like that of al-Husayn, ended in disaster: he was killed, decapitated and crucified on a pole. However, his end is not described in the heart-rending manner of al-Husayn's. The reason seems to be the many warnings Zayd had received about the Kufans' unreliable character, so that he had better knowledge about them than al-Husayn, and should have made the rational decision not to rebel, even if his case was not treated in the best way by the caliph and his governor. Nevertheless, the greatest sinners in moral terms are the caliph's men who took part in the killing of another member of the Prophet's family. This is dramatized in the poems Tabari cites. The caliph's governor sent Zayd's head to Madina, as a warning to his family, and a poet stood up before it and recited:

O violator of the covenant {(*mīthāq*)},
rejoice in what has brought you disaster!
You have violated the {contract (ʿ*ahd*)} and the covenant {(*mīthāq*)},
you are steeped in wrongdoing.
Satan has broken faith
over what he promised you.

But the people of Madina responded, shutting him up:

You poet of evil,
you have become a liar!
Are you reviling the son of the Messenger of God,
just to gratify those who govern you?
May God confound you,
morning and evening!
And on the Day of Gathering, make no mistake,
the fire will be your abode! (Ibid, 52–3)

The Umayyad caliphate was eventually brought down through a concerted propaganda campaign by the Prophet's family, the Banu Hashim, which included both the 'Abbasid and the 'Alid branches (*History*, vol. 27). Up until the actual *coup d'état* in 749, the two branches were united in the cause to reclaim the caliphate for the Prophet's family. The people of Kufa were then an important support base, and the vast Iranian province of Khurasan. However, once the Umayyads' power was decisively broken, the 'Abbasids got the upper hand over the 'Alids and forced them out of the caliphate (vols. 27 and 28). When the first 'Abbasid caliph, Abu l-'Abbas 'al-Saffah' ('The Spiller of Blood'), assumed power, he delivered his inaugural address, in a strategic attempt to secure this stronghold of pro-'Alid sentiment, in Kufa's mosque, where 'Ali had been killed by the Khariji conspirator. His speech makes no mention of old betrayals, only promises of a brighter future, and a discreet threat:

> People of Kufa, you are the halting-place of our love, the lodging of our affections. You it is who remained steadfast, you who were not deflected from our love by the injustice of the people of tyranny against you until you reached our epoch and God brought you our revolution. You of all mankind are most fortunate in us and most worthy of our generosity. We have increased your allowances to a hundred dirhams. Make ready, then, for I am the manifest Spiller (*Saffāḥ*), the desolating Avenger. (*History*, xxvii/ Williams. 154)

The 'Abbasid take-over meant that the 'Alids were once again reduced to royalty with rights to allowance but not state power. The circumstances were awkward for both parties: the 'Alids always carried the spiritual legitimacy of being the Prophet's next of kin, while the 'Abbasids always knew that they had come to power with the help of the 'Alids and then betrayed them, which made them paranoid and suspicious of their loyalty.

There was, however, one noticeable attempt by the 'Abbasids to put an 'Alid on the throne. This was when the caliph al-Ma'mun (r. 813–33; *History*, vol. 32) appointed the 'Alid al-Rida as his heir in the year 817, and ordered the court to change the official colours from the 'Abbasid black to the 'Alid green. The reason was pragmatic: before becoming caliph, al-Ma'mun had been governor of Khurasan, the rich Iranian province which supported the 'Abbasid revolution, and thereafter provided large tax revenues and the bulk of al-Ma'mun's loyal troops, the so-called 'sons of the dynasty' (*abnā' al-dawla*), who were descendants of the first Arab conquerors of this region. These troops stationed in Baghdad retained a Khurasanian identity. Now, al-Ma'mun had seized the caliphate from his brother al-Amin, who had his support base in Baghdad and in Syrian army contingents. The majority of Baghdad's population and the 'Abbasid court resented al-Ma'mun's take-over, and so al-Ma'mun relied heavily on the Khurasanians for support. As there was much pro-'Alid sentiment in Khurasan, dating back to the Hashimi campaign against the Umayyads, it made sense for al-Ma'mun to appoint an 'Alid as successor. However, other members of the 'Abbasid royal family and the Baghdad populace refused to accept this appointment, broke their allegiance to al-Ma'mun and appointed another caliph, Ibrahim al-Mahdi; the affair ended with al-Rida's death in 818, and al-Ma'mun's recantation and continuation as caliph.

As well as appointing an 'Alid as heir, al-Ma'mun took upon himself the authority to pronounce on doctrinal matters, thus turning the secular authority of the caliphate into a political-and-spiritual power in the manner of the 'Alid *Imam*s. In early 833 he proclaimed the Mu'tazili doctrine of the Qur'an's being created as the doctrine that all judges and theologians of Baghdad must profess, and he purged those who adhered to Ahmad b. Hanbal's belief in the Qur'an as God's eternal, uncreated Word. Thus ensued the *miḥna* or 'inquisition' (*History*, xxxii/Bosworth. 199–230). Tabari frames this episode in an interesting way, by first describing how al-Ma'mun initiated a military campaign against the Byzantines, which required vast levies of troops and, of course, taxes to pay them. Only then does he proceed to the 'inquisition', giving the impression that the campaign somehow required purging the judiciary. The narrative about the trial begins with a long speech in which the caliph justifies his measures:

God has made incumbent upon the imāms and caliphs of the Muslims that they should be zealous in establishing God's religion, which He has asked them to guard faithfully; in the heritage of prophethood of which He has made them inheritors; in the tradition of knowledge which He has entrusted to their keeping; in acting justly with the government of their subjects; and in being diligent in obeying God's will in their conduct towards those subjects. (Ibid, 199–200)

The caliph goes on to argue that it is only because of the lowly ignorance of the masses that such an unfounded idea as the Qur'an being God's eternal Word could take hold, as the Qur'an itself says that it has been *'made'* by God; accordingly the enlightened caliph must step in and pronounce a doctrinal verdict (ibid, 200–2). Al-Ma'mun proceeds to compare the belief that the Qur'an is God's eternal Word with the Christian belief that Jesus is God's uncreated Word – also interesting in light of his having just launched a campaign against the Christian Byzantines (ibid, 207). Further, the speech Tabari reports shows that the doctrinal charge against judges and governors believing in the eternal Qur'an was coupled with accusations of keeping tax revenue for themselves, and charging usury (which prompts another association with Christianity): '[T]hey have added polytheism to their practice of usury and have become just like the Christians' (ibid, 218). It thus seems plausible that Tabari thought that the campaign against Byzantium and the purging of certain judges and governors were connected, at least in the accusations of withholding tax revenue at a time of war and adhering to allegedly un-Islamic or 'Christian' doctrines.

One may ask what Tabari thought about the caliph's assumption of the right to promulgate doctrine, 'in the heritage of prophethood'? He does not say anything explicit about it. However, in a completely different context, recounting 'Some of [the] meritorious deeds not previously recorded' of 'Umar b. al-Khattab, he reported, from Ibn Ishaq and Ibn 'Abbas:

As ʿUmar b. al-Khaṭṭāb and some of his friends were reciting poetry together, one said that so-and-so was the best poet. Another said that so-and-so was the best poet. (Ibn ʿAbbās) continued: I arrived and ʿUmar remarked, 'The most knowledgeable on the subject has just arrived.' {…} [ʿUmar] said, 'Do you know, Ibn ʿAbbās, what kept your people from [being put] over [Quraysh] after Muḥammad's death?' I did not want to answer, so I said, 'If I do not know, then the Commander of the Faithful will tell me.' ʿUmar said, 'They were unwilling for you to combine the prophethood and the caliphate, lest you magnify yourselves above your own people and be proud. Quraysh made the choice for themselves; they were right and have been granted success.' (*History*, xiv/Smith. 136–7)

Since Tabari counts this among 'Umar's 'meritorious deeds', he may have agreed with 'Umar's criticism of 'combining the prophethood and the caliphate', that is, assuming both spiritual and political authority. 'Umar's words indeed read like a prophecy of al-Ma'mun's speech, where he claims himself to be in the prophetic tradition, and declares his intellectual superiority over the people. Moreover, 'Ali b. 'Isa's vizieral policy was to reduce tax pressure by refraining from war campaigns; to the extent that Tabari agreed with this, he would have been opposed to al-Ma'mun's campaign.

Al-Ma'mun died in the beginning of 834. In his deathbed speech, he expressed concerns for the 'Alids similar to what we have seen in Tabari's accounts of 'Alid rebellions, namely that their rights should be respected:

[In regard to] these, your paternal cousins who are the descendants of the Commander of the Faithful ʿAlī b. Abī Ṭālib [the ʿAlids], make them welcome in your court circle, overlook the transgressions of those who act wrongly and welcome those who act honestly. Do not neglect giving them presents each year on the appropriate occasions, for the rights due to them demand recognition on several grounds of consideration. (*History*, xxxii/Bosworth. 230)

The inquisition and enforced doctrine about the created Qur'an were abolished by the caliph al-Mutawakkil in 848. However, troubles with the 'Alids continued, in spite of al-

Ma'mun's wise counsel. In the year 864–65, Zayd's grandson Yahya b. 'Umar revolted in Kufa. According to Tabari, the cause of his rebellion was that he was indebted and hard-pressed by his creditors. He approached the 'Abbasid governor in charge of the 'Alids' affairs in Kufa for a grant, but was turned down in an offensive manner. Yahya made things worse by cursing the governor in his assembly. Then he was imprisoned until his family bailed him out. Still in financial difficulty, he left for Baghdad, and contacted the administration there for an allowance, but was again rudely turned down: 'Why should there be an allowance for the likes of you?' (*History*, xxxv/Saliba. 15). Then he left for Kufa, gathered a mixed force of Bedouins, liberated prison inmates, and Shi'i sympathizers, managed to rob the treasury, and declared war on the 'Abbasid authorities. His revolt gained widespread support. The 'Abbasid governor in Kufa was appointed by the Tahirids, a powerful family of vassals based in Khurasan. They ordered the rebellion quelled by force. Eventually, Yahya was killed and his head sent around for display. One of Yahya's 'Alid relatives happened to be in the Tahirid vassal's assembly as the latter was celebrating the killing of Yahya. The 'Alid exclaimed: 'O Prince! You are being congratulated for killing a man for whom the Messenger of God, had he been alive, would have been among the bereaved' (ibid, 20). Tabari cites another 'Alid's response in verse, which again, as in earlier narratives about the killing of an 'Alid, ends with the threat of divine retribution:

O Banū Ṭāhir eat him like a plague
  for the flesh of the prophet is not nourishing.
A revenge that God Himself seeks
  will, I am sure, be crowned with perfect success. (Ibid)

Tabari's presentation of the affair brings out its complexity. Yahya's rebellion was understandable in that he had been denied an allowance. Equally understandable was the Tahirids' need to suppress the rebellion. However, the killing of another member of the Prophet's family was not justified. The first link in this chain of events was the refusal to lend him the money he needed. A just and prudent functionary would not have done so, because denying help to someone in need inevitably provokes some drastic measure.

Immediately after Yahya's rebellion, another broke out in 864 in Tabaristan, led by the 'Alid al-Hasan b. Zayd. The reason, Tabari explains, was that the Tahirid vassal had been granted some lands in Tabaristan as a reward for killing Yahya and putting down his rebellion in Kufa. Adjacent to those lands was a plot 'jointly utilized by the people of that district as source of firewood, and for grazing lands and pasturage for their animals. No one held ownership of this area; it was but a barren stretch of uncultivated state land, except for thickets, some bushes and grazing grass' (ibid, 21). This land was, in other words, set aside for public use, just as Khusraw Anushirwan and 'Umar b. al-Khattab had set aside some parts of the Sawad for public use. Tabaristan was already ruled by a governor appointed by the Tahirids in Khurasan. This governor and his two sons were very unpopular; as Tabari puts it, if the story of their 'excesses were properly told, it would fill a book by itself' (ibid). When the Tahirid envoy came to take possession of the lands, he also claimed the uncultivated common used by the people, in spite of the fact that it was not included in the assigned fief. This triggered a broad uprising against Tahirid governorship, in which the people of Tabaristan and the neighbouring region of Daylam, swore allegiance to the 'Alid al-Hasan b. Zayd, who resided in al-Rayy. Al-Hasan b. Zayd managed to take control of the whole region of Tabaristan and parts of western Iran up to the city of Hamadhan. His rule lasted until 928, which means that Tabaristan was under the rule of this 'Alid family for most of Tabari's professional life.

While Tabari judged this 'Alid, al-Hasan b. Zayd, to be a better leader in Tabaristan than the Tahirids, his judgement was not based on partiality. He could also be critical of 'Alids. About one who was appointed governor over Kufa in 866–67, he writes that he 'reportedly devastated the regions around Kufa, causing harm to people while seizing their possessions and estates', and approves the decision of the 'Abbasid authorities' to have him peacefully deposed (ibid, 142). It seems to have been an important concern for Tabari that wrongdoing should be dealt with appropriately, without giving rise to new problems.

One of Tabari's reports in his narrative for the year 895–96 under the rule of al-Mu'tadid illustrates that concern very well. The report was about the 'Alid ruler of Tabaristan and the fact that he had sent great sums of money to another 'Alid, Muhammad b. Ward, for the latter to distribute among his followers in Baghdad, Kufa, Makka, and Madina. The 'Abbasid governor Badr found out about this and called in Muhammad b. Ward for questioning, denouncing what he had done. Muhammad b. Ward explained that this was nothing unusual. The governor then informed the caliph al-Mu'tadid that the man and his money was in his custody, and asked what al-Mu'tadid wanted him to do. Al-Mu'tadid then told his governor about a dream he had had after his father al-Nasir had appointed him as his successor. In this dream al-Mu'tadid meets a man who identifies himself as 'Ali b. Abi Talib, prophesies the number of al-Mu'tadid's descendants who will become caliphs, and urges him to 'be good to my descendants'. Al-Mu'tadid then concludes: 'So release the money and release the man, and tell him to write to his master in Ṭabāristān that anything he sends him he should send to him openly. Muḥammad b. Ward shall distribute whatever he does openly. Also, help Muḥammad to do as he wishes in this connection!' (*History*, xxxviii/ Rosenthal. 25).

The moral here seems to be that if matters are handled professionally (which, as well as upholding people's rights, includes transparency and accountability in matters of state and administration) the causes of rebellions and the ensuing destruction of life and property can be removed. A final example of the importance Tabari assigned to 'upholding rights' is found among the events reported for 915, the last year of the *History*. He comments on the rule in Tabaristan of the 'Alid, al-Hasan b. 'Ali al-Utrush: 'People had never seen anything like al-Uṭrūsh's justice, his exemplary way of life, and the way he {*upheld rights* (*iqāmatihi al-ḥaqq*)}.' (Ibid, 204)[1]

As it drew to a close, Tabari's *History* rapidly thins out; the last years are chronicled through what appear to be more or less random reports about the irreversible decline of the 'Abbasid state. Duri has suggested that this was because Tabari viewed history 'as an expression of divine will and a depository for experiences'.[2] Thus, if Tabari wrote the *History* as guidance for state administrators, the decisive 'case-experiences' had already been described, in the *History*'s outline, long before the last few years which merely confirmed that the rational ways to run the state had not been chosen.

---

[1] Rosenthal (ibid, 205, n. 971) translates *iqāmatihi al-ḥaqq* as 'the way he established truth', and has the following note on this sentence: ' "Established truth" seems here to reflect a Shīʿite notion. The sentence, found in {other manuscripts}, may have been intentionally omitted by the scribe of the prototype of {this manuscript}. If Ṭabarī in fact used it, it was probably an expression of local pride. He would hardly have endorsed a Shīʿite pretender in such glowing terms for any other reason.' I translate *iqāmatihi al-ḥaqq* as 'upheld rights' – *ḥaqq* can mean both 'truth' and 'right' in the legal sense – because Tabari's comment can then be read as referring to al-Utrush's administrative practice of upholding people's legal rights, rather than the Shiʿi concept of esoteric truth. That is consonant with Tabari's support for anyone who upheld people's rights, and does not need to imply either Shiʿi partisanship or 'local pride'.

[2] Duri, *Historical Writing*, 71.

Part 4

Conclusion

Tabari's general theory of language, which he presents in the *Jami'*, in particular the subjective, personal dimension of 'explanation' (interpretation), has not previously been explored. In this book, I have sought to apply the notion that there is always a personal dimension to explanations, to the *History*: to define what we can, with good reason, infer were Tabari's personal concerns, and to trace them in the *History*'s narratives. Doing so should contribute to our understanding of Tabari's stance on such subjects as state administration and relations between the state and the 'Alids.

Regarding the state, I have concluded that Tabari had an overarching concern to rescue the disintegrating 'Abbasid state. This concern is consistently reflected in his analysis of which policies strengthened and which weakened imperial states. He seems to have favoured a policy of centralized and bureaucratized taxation and re-distribution, and, on appointment to government office, of personal merit over kinship. In both cases his preferred policy is one founded on 'rule of law', and the corollary of transparency and accountability. As for the 'Alids, Tabari was concerned, in line with his general concern for 'rule of law', that their rights should be protected by the state administration: as descendants of the Prophet's family, they had rights as 'royalty' according to the social contract between them and the ruling ʿAbbasids. If this concern for the lawful rights of the ʿAlids is added to the ʿsemi-rationalist' position that he shared with the Jaʿfari Imami Shiʿa, it is easy to see how, in the eyes of the Hanbalis, he might be perceived as 'pro-Alid'. However, we have seen that Tabari was not 'pro' anyone; he measured all alike against the same standard of rationality. This rationality on his part was tempered by profound empathy – for example, one of the main arguments in favour of a rationally administered tax system was that it secured the needs of every social group, including peasants and labourers like the Zanj.

Another personal concern we should expect to find in the *History* is the importance for him of his home province Tabaristan. This concern is not expressed in the number but in the weight of his references to Tabaristan, in the sense that these references occur in significant contexts. The first example occurs in what I called the 'Mythological Prelude' to the *History* (see above, pp. 70, 77), where he treats the foundation of Persian kingship and the related creation myth about the f first man, Jayumart. According to the myth as cited by Tabari, this Jayumart lived on Mt Dunbawand in Tabaristan, from where he ruled over the territories of Fars and Mesopotamia or Babylon. Although these were, in terms of agricultural output and potential tax revenue, the two most important regions for the Persian dynasties, Tabari nevertheless cited a myth that locates the origins of Persian kingship in Tabaristan. The second instance is where Tabari narrates the ominous sixth year in ʿUthman's reign, in which he lost the Prophet's signet ring and things took a turn towards disaster. Just before the incident of the ring, ʿUthman's commander conquered Tabaristan, and although the Arab Muslims defeated 'idolaters', Tabari pointedly narrates reports that present the conquerors as ruthless plunderers, and ridiculous at that (see above, p. 109). This is important for our appreciation of the significant space and role Tabari assigned to Persian kingship. Political history begins with their kings, who were just as rational or irrational as the Muslim caliphs after them, so that there is nothing in the *History* to indicate that Islamic caliphate was inherently superior to other forms of government. The third example is from 914–15, the very last year chronicled by Tabari. He describes the rule in Tabaristan of the 'Alid al-'Utrush as a model of 'good governance', protecting the rights of everyone. Thus he closes the *History* with an 'Alid in Tabaristan as exemplary of rational government, at the same time that the 'Abbasid state was a shambles (see above, p. 144).

As Tabari had hoped, his works have had lasting influence. This is especially true for the *History* and the *Jami'*, his major and comprehensive *opera*, which have reached us complete. The Persian Samanid vizier Bal'ami in 963 ordered the *History* and the *Jami'* to be translated into Persian and reworked into abridged versions. This may have been because he deemed Tabari's political, legal and theological approach to be what the Samanid emirate needed to defend itself against the sectarian religious and political adversaries it was facing at the time.[1] Sadly, we do not know to what extent the Ottoman rulers who kept copies of the *History* in their library consulted it. However, we know more about its role in scholarship. As already mentioned, it has remained the most consulted and, in Islamic scholarship, the most authoritative, source on Sassanid and early Islamic history. The *Jami'* is equally important. It enjoys unrivalled status as the *summa* of the first generations of Qur'an exegesis and has held its place in the theological curricula in the Islamic world.

As for epistemology and theological doctrine, Tabari represented, it seems, the 'semi-rationalist' synthesis between Mu'tazili rationalism and Hanbali empiricism later associated

---

1 See Elton Daniel, 'The Samanid "Translations" '.

with al-Ash'ari (d. *ca.* 935) and the Ash'ari school, which came to dominate Sunni theology, its most famous medieval proponent al-Ghazzali (d. 1111) being, like Tabari, a Shafi'i in legal theory.

And yet, in spite of Tabari's fame, and with a lapse of some 1100 years since his death, research on both the *History* and *Jami'* is in important respects still in its infancy. Their contents are surely well-known to scholars within the classical Islamic sciences, so it is mainly non-Arabic speakers outside the Islamic disciplines who struggle to understand their full implications. This is partly because very few non-native speakers master Arabic sufficiently well to be able to survey Tabari's vast works. With the recent completion of the scholarly English translation of the *History*, there will no doubt be an upsurge in new studies. The fact that only fractions of the *Jami'* have been translated means that it is not accessible to most students and younger scholars. This has in all likelihood restricted research on Tabari's theology, which is to a large extent contained in his Qur'an commentary. It seems to me that its proximity to al-Ash'ari's synthesis deserves more attention than it has received so far, as do his theories of language and interpretation.

A few words may also be said about the implications of Tabari's *History* for Islamic political philosophy. There were no Islamic political theorists similar to Plato or Aristotle, who defined in general terms the rights and duties of rulers and citizens/subjects. However, Tabari's presentation through concrete historical examples in the *History* of the Qur'anic concepts of covenant (*mīthāq*) and contract (*ʿahd*) may be of relevance in this regard. While not linked up as a philosophical treatise with formal definition of terms and abstract general principles, the concrete examples do appear to have a consistent theory behind them. Even though there is no immediately evident Islamic equivalent of the classical Greek concept of 'citizen', 'Muslim' as a term refers to the one who is symbolically subject to God, and practically to the state and the law, with particular rights and duties; and 'the people of the written document' (*ahl al-kitāb*) are the non-Muslims bound by contract to the state, also with particular rights and duties. Thus it is possible to see in the Qur'anic terminology, as deployed by Tabari, different categories of subjects or, in the case of Muslims, 'citizens', with legally defined rights.[1]

From this it may be tempting to jump to the conclusion, as have modern Islamists of diverse persuasions, that 'the Qur'an is a constitution'. It is not. The Qur'an is a writing which *describes* the *constitutional principle* of 'covenant'; while the covenant is described in the Qur'an, it is not identical with the Qur'anic text, or with any historically particular law or political framework. This is very clear from Tabari's *History*, where the covenant is implemented as 'constitution' first by the Persian kings (who of course did not have the Qur'an), and the Israelites, and later by the Muslims. By demonstrating the universal validity of legal rights and obligations for rulers and subjects, Tabari comes across, while being a devout believer, as an Enlightenment thinker: had there been in reality such a phenomenon as 'the Oriental despot', described critically by Montesquieu in

---

1 This approach to Tabari's *History* opens up new perspectives on its possible significance for Ibn Khaldun's *Muqaddima*, or 'Introduction' to Islamic history. Ibn Khaldun theorized the relationship between the state and the tribes as one of dialectical tension, the state representing merit and abstract legal principles, and the tribe family solidarity. Tabari did not theorize this tension, but his reports about the Prophet and the Companion caliphs bring it out through factual detail: when 'Uthman favoured his kin, it was a resurgence of tribal rationality and expectations against the law and merit-based rationality of the state. On Ibn Khaldun's referring to the *History* for information, see Khalidi, *Arabic Historical Thought*, esp. p. 227.

L'Esprit des lois (1748) as a ruler above the law, Tabari would have agreed with the critique.

5

Further reading

My recommendations are necessarily limited, in this introduction to Tabari for the general reader, to studies that are written in English, though I do allow myself to mention a couple of the most useful works in French and German. Most regrettably, I have had to exclude studies in Arabic, Persian, Urdu and Turkish.[1] (Bibliographical details of the works mentioned here are given in the Bibliography section.)

---

1 The suggested readings have Tabari and his work as their main focus. One exception is Aziz al-Azmeh's recent collection of essays, *The Times of History: Universal Topics in Islamic Historiography* (2007). Although Tabari is one of many sources in *The Times of History*, it discusses issues directly relevant to the subjects taken up in this book. Taken together, al-Azmeh's essays show how, at different times in history and junctures in historiography, the ideas and methods of Muslim thinkers and historians correspond to those of their counterparts among ancient Greek or medieval Jewish and Christian or contemporary European and American thinkers and scholars. On the particular issue of government, it becomes clear both that Muslims' theories of government change through history and that they, at each historical time, share the main characteristics of their counterparts in the 'other cultures'.

On the life of Tabari. The best starting-point for an overview of Tabari's life and works is C. E. Bosworth's article 'al-Ṭabarī' in *Encyclopaedia of Islam.* It surveys the main research problems and the major biographical sources. Bosworth (the translator of vol. 5 of the *History* on the Sassanid *shahs*) suggests that Tabari was of Persian descent on his mother's side. That is also the view taken by Franz-Christoph Muth (1983). Franz Rosenthal, in 'The Life and Works of al-Tabari' (*History*, i. 5–154), disagrees with the Persian descent theory. In his much fuller study, which has a detailed bibliography of Tabari's works, Rosenthal has a section (135–54) about the English translation, and a brief account of how the *History* has been received in the West and of earlier translations. He also covers biographical records on the Jariri school, and the controversy between Tabari and the Hanbalis, albeit downplaying the latter's opposition to him.

On Tabari's jurisprudence and theology. Compared to the attention given to the *History*, there are relatively few detailed studies of Tabari's other major works. Bosworth and Rosenthal's biographies include general descriptions of Tabari's positions in theology and law. Christopher Melchert's study, *The Formation of the Sunni Schools of Law* (1997), contains a few very good pages (191–7) on Tabari's 'semi-rationalism', including information about the short-lived Jariri school. Particularly interesting, for the debate surrounding Hanbali allegations of Tabari's Shi'i sympathies, is Melchert's observation that Tabari's Shafi'i 'semi-rationalism' put him in the same legal theoretical position as the Twelver Shi'i Ja'fari school. Yasir Ibrahim's *al-Tabari's Book of Jihad* (2007) gives a good view of Tabari's method in the *Ikhtilaf*, and its introduction has an interesting discussion on differences between classical and modern legal opinions on *jihad.* Dominique Sourdel's introduction to his translation of *Sarih al-sunna* ('Une Profession de Foi', 1968), gives a good account of Tabari's doctrinal positions; he holds, unlike Rosenthal, that the Hanbalis were a problem and this provoked Tabari's writing of the creed as defensive apology.

On Tabari's hermeneutics and Qur'an commentary. There are partial translations of the *Jami'*: an abridged, annotated French translation of the *Jami'* up to Q. 4. 176 by Pierre Godé (1986); one in English as far as Q. 2. 103 by John Cooper (1987) also contains an abridged translation of Tabari's methodological introduction. On Tabari's 'commentary by the exegetical tradition', two useful articles comparing his *tafsīr bi-l-maʾthūr* with that of Ibn Kathir (d. 1373) are Jane D. McAuliffe's 'Quranic Hermeneutics' (1988) and Norman Calder's '*Tafsir* from Tabari to Ibn Kathir' (1993). Ibn Kathir streamlined Tabari's work by summarizing all the divergent interpretations that Tabari had reported. McAuliffe sees this as an indication of progress in the discipline; Calder sees it as marking the demise of critical exegesis in favour of producing a uniform understanding of the Qur'an. (In modern times, the latter typifies the so-called 'Salafi' approach to the sources.) Alongside Calder's study, Uri Rubin's essay (1993) on Tabari's treatment of 'the seven *mathani*' (Q. 15. 87), 'Exegesis and *Hadith*', also addresses the broader question of whether Tabari's *tafsīr bi-l-maʾthūr* excluded a personal, creative approach. Rubin argues that Tabari categorized and evaluated the exegetical traditions in a way which suggests that his personal interpretation of the verse preceded and determined his evaluation of the traditions. In the same 1993 volume, Abdolkader Tayob's 'An analytical survey of al-Tabari's exegesis' demonstrates Tabari's personal contributions in interpretation of the Qur'anic concept of *fitna*: unlike later interpretations of *fitna* as divisive of the community and therefore evil, Tabari in some contexts saw *fitna* as a necessary test of faith and morals. Tayob explains this in terms of Tabari's engagement in the social and political issues of his day.

Unrivalled on Tabari's hermeneutics and theology is Claude Gilliot's *Exégèse, langue et théologie en Islam: L'Exégèse coranique de Tabari* (1990), which includes a survey of all Tabari's works. This book, given Gilliot's attention to detail, is one for the dedicated reader. Its main focus is the role of language theory, in particular the special 'qualities' (Gilliot's rendering of *maʿani*) that distinguish the divine language of the Qur'an from ordinary language. Gilliot argues that Tabari's principal aim as commentator was theological, namely to expound the Qur'an's qualities as divine speech.

On Tabari's History. Most studies of Tabari are devoted to the *History*, a testament to its enduring status in Islamic scholarly tradition as the definitive history of early Islam. Important information specific to the epoch and subject-matter of each volume is found in its 'Translator's Foreword'. The survey below is organized roughly according to the major debates about the *History* and Tabari's methodology.

European Orientalists were aware of the *History*'s reputation as early as the seventeenth century, notably the Frenchman Barthélémy d'Herbelot (1625–95), who wrote an entry on it in his encyclopaedia *Bibliothèque Orientale*. Franz-Christoph Muth's *Die Annalen von at-Tabari im Spiegel der europäischen Bearbeitungen* (1983) is a valuable survey of European studies of the *History*, listing the different editions and translations. It shows that research moved sharply forward with the Leiden edition supervised by de Goeje.

A member of de Goeje's team, the German Orientalist Theodor Nöldeke, translated and commented on parts of Tabari's narrative on the Sassanid period under the title *Geschichte der Perser und Araber zur Zeit der Sasaniden* (1879, repr. 1973). Nöldeke's introduction gives a detailed account of Tabari's main sources for the period and related subjects. It also puts forward views (see p. xiii) that still appear in studies of Tabari's methodology: that Tabari was primarily concerned with theological matters, that he was not a critical analyst of history but an extraordinarily assiduous compiler of source material and (insofar as his sources were accurate) reporter of facts. Rosenthal, in his early studies, drew the same conclusions: see 'The Influence of the Biblical Tradition on Muslim Historiography' (1962), and his classic *A History of Muslim Historiography* (1952 [1968]), where Tabari's *History* is implied in Rosenthal's sections on the *khabar* form. Similarly, Gilliot in 'Mythe, recit, histoire du salut dans le commentaire coranique de Tabari' (1994) sees a theological conception of history and the community in Tabari's Qur'an commentary as also in his *History*. Chase Robinson is the most recent proponent of this view, in his primer *Islamic Historiography* (2003; pp. 134–8, esp. 137); more in passing, Roberto Tottolli too has characterized Tabari's work as essentially religious and 'remote from the modern concept of the discipline of history', in his primer *Biblical Prophets in the Qur'an and Muslim Literature* (2002; p. 129).

Other scholars have emphasized the role of Qur'anic concepts for Tabari's *History* without seeing this as opposed to a scholarly-critical approach and, indeed, arguing that there is a congruence between the Qur'an commentary and the *History*. For example, in 'Qur'anic Myth and Narrative Structure' (1989), Stephen Humphreys studied the way Tabari structured the *History* according to a Qur'anic, cyclical pattern of Covenant, Betrayal and Redemption, both in its overall outline and in individual narratives, exemplified by the murder of 'Uthman. Tarif Khalidi, in the section on 'Tabari the 'imam' of *Hadith* historiography' in his very accessible *Arabic Historical Thought in the Classical Period* (1994; pp. 73–81), shows the paradigmatic, 'theological' function of Adam and Satan in the *History*, and how Tabari shaped historical narrative so as to present Islam and the caliphate as inheriting Israelite prophethood and Iranian kingship. Also departing from the Qur'an as the source of early Islamic conceptions of history, Fred Donner's broad study of the common themes in early Islamic historical writings, *Narratives of Islamic Origins* (1998), contains a brief survey of the thematic contents of the *History*. Donner's comparative approach enables a good understanding of which common historical themes were of particular interest to Tabari.

Bernd Radtke's 'Towards a Typology of Abbasid Universal Chronicles' (1990) is a reflection on the cosmologies informing 'Abbasid universal histories, including Tabari's. Radtke compares them to a late antique Christian Nestorian and Monophysite genre of 'historicized exegesis'. He also floats the idea that the linear concept of time, with a definite beginning and end, is typical of the religious scholars (Tabari included), compared to the cyclical time frame of histories written by the 'secular' scribes.

Another broad debate concerns the *khabar* form of history, which Tabari's typifies. Nöldeke and the early Rosenthal represent an early phase in *khabar* and Tabari studies, in which the focus was on the fact that knowledge was always transmitted, rather than (as is claimed for modern Western history writing) creatively processed by the historian. The great Biblical scholar and Orientalist Julius Wellhausen shared this view, although he was more appreciative of Tabari's skills in selecting his sources. He wrote a history from the Prophet to the 'Abbasids, *Das arabische Reich und sein Sturz* (1902; 'The Arab Kingdom and its Fall'), in which he argued that the 'Abbasid *coup d'état* effectively transferred imperial power back to the Persians, because Islamicized Persians it was who constituted the decisive force of the 'Abbasids' revolution and its staying power. The reports in Tabari's *History* were among his main sources; he was especially appreciative of Abu Mikhnaf's qualities as both historian and prose writer, and correspondingly disparaging about Sayf b. 'Umar, whose reports he saw as biased copies of other historians' efforts.

Wellhausen perhaps initiated the trend of looking at the differences within Tabari's source material, and his arrangement of it. Examples of such studies are the Tabari chapters in E. L. Petersen's *Ali and Mu'awiya in Early Arabic Tradition* (1964), and Marshal Hodgson's groundbreaking article 'Two Pre-Modern Historians' (1968). Both Petersen and Hodgson shifted attention from the nature of the *khabar* form to Tabari's interweaving and juxtaposition of the *akhbar* with his own comments, arguing that Tabari's narrative was not just compilation but proper historical writing. Petersen and Hodgson, focusing on the murder of 'Uthman and, in its aftermath, the challenges facing 'Ali, show how Tabari juxtaposed the reports of Sayf b. 'Umar (who idealized all the Companions) and al-Waqidi (who related 'Uthman's mistakes and the grievances they gave rise to). In the same vein Joseph Bradin Roberts' PhD. thesis 'Early Islamic Historiography' (1986), and Humphreys' 'Qur'anic Myth and Narrative Structure in Early Islamic Historiography' (1989), argued that Tabari held al-Waqidi to be the historically accurate source, and included the Sayf material only to illustrate a religiously idealized view for the less discerning reader.

That view has recently been challenged by Boaz Shoshan in *Poetics of Islamic Historiography: Deconstructing Tabari's History* (2004), following up on Ella Landau-Tasseron's 'Sayf Ibn 'Umar in Medieval and Modern Scholarship' (1990). From a close reading of reports about the murder of 'Uthman, Shoshan suggests (pp. 173–208) that Tabari regarded neither al-Waqidi nor Sayf's reports as more accurate, and used the latter to convey the appropriate response to the murder of 'Uthman, namely despair and disgust, regardless of the caliph's mistakes. A similar analysis of Tabari's use of Sayf's reports is Abdelkadir Tayob's 'Tabari on the Companions of the Prophet' (1999), on the Battle of the Camel. An original study of Tabari's narrative about the killing of al-Husayn by Torsten Hylén (the PhD thesis, 'Husayn, the Mediator';

2007) deploys a structuralist myth-analysis (inspired by Claude Lévi-Strauss) to Tabari's reports from Abu Mikhnaf. Hylén concludes that Tabari held that Muslims should have followed al-Husayn in the case of his conflict with the Umayyad Yazid b. Mu'awiya. A sub-set of such studies focus on Tabari's use of Biblical motifs to make the Prophet and Islam the fulfilment of Biblical prophecies, notably: Gilliot, 'Mythe, recit, histoire du salut' (1994), and 'al-Tabari and the "History of Salvation" ' (2008); Mårtensson, 'Discourse and Historical Analysiss' (2005); and McAuliffe, 'Al-Tabari's Prelude to the Prophet' (2008).

The most recent contribution of this kind is the volume *Al-Tabari: A Medieval Muslim Historian and His Work* (2008). It is edited by Hugh Kennedy, with an Introduction by Tarif Khalidi, and contains important specialist studies of the sources Tabari used in the different sections of the *History*; of the relationship between the *History* and other historical works; and of editions and translations of the *History* and the *Jami'*. Regarding Tabari's sources, contributions include e.g. the pre-Islamic prophets and the Biblical material (Michael Whitby; McAuliffe), the Persian kings and Byzantium (Mohsin Zakeri; Zeev Rubin; John Howard-Johnston), Shi'i sources (Sebastian Günther), Abbasid sources (Kennedy), Tabari's biographical works (Ella Landau-Tasseron). Translations of the *History*, and its relationship to other historical works, is treated by Walter Kaegi and Paul Cobb (Heraclius and Tabari), Khalil Athamina (al-Baladhuri and Tabari), Ralph-Johannes Lilie (Theophanes and Tabari), Chase Robinson (al-Azdi and Tabari). As for studies of translations and editions, these include the Samanid Persian translation (Elton Daniel), Russian translations (Anas Khalidov), and the Leiden edition (Arnoud Vrolijk). The volume concludes with a tribute to Tabari's work by Osman Ismail al-Bili.

There are still very few monographs which seek to grasp the entire *History*. The earliest, Tayeb el-Hibri's *Reinterpreting*

Islamic Historiography (1999b), follows on his brief article 'The Unity of Tabari's Chronicle' (1999a). The article lays out the argument that informs the book, namely that certain narrative structures (e.g., Cain's murder of his brother Abel) run through and shape the *History*. The book applies this approach to the narratives about the caliphs Harun al-Rashid, his sons al-Amin and al-Ma'mun, and al-Mutawakkil, and argues that these narratives cannot be used as information about the actual events: they are not neutral reports but reflections on ethical, administrative–political issues that the caliphs are made to exemplify – they tell us what historians like Tabari thought about the politics of their day, not about the actual political events.

Shoshan's *Poetics of Islamic Historiography* (2004) is a critical response to El-Hibri. Reading closely Tabari's reports on four historical events (the appointment of Abu Bakr; the murder of 'Uthman; the Battle of Siffin; and the killing of al-Husayn), and using the classical concept of *mimesis* ('imitation in order to represent something'), Shoshan argues that both Tabari and his sources reported historical events mimetically, with extreme attention to detail. By juxtaposing reports as he did, Tabari gave to events the meaning that he intended, while the historical information conveyed by the sources remains factual.

My own article 'Discourse and Historical Analysis' (2005), building on Michel de Certeau's discourse analysis in *The Writing of History* (1988), tried to develop an objectively applicable method for reading the *History*. It shows how Tabari's personal concerns can be identified in the *History*, and whether it offers historical analysis or moral evaluations. That method has been followed in this book, extended from the article's focus on systems of land tax to the *History* as a whole. By reconstructing Tabari's personal concerns, with the help of biographical information and historical information about the problems the state administration was facing in his time, it becomes possible to discover Tabari's analysis and personal shaping of history.

Overall, it seems from these suggested readings, that Tabari has enabled his readers over the generations to get a rather good view of him and his concerns amidst the complex politics of Baghdad of his day. I think it fair to say that the view of him we get is a most flattering one.

BIBLIOGRAPHY

Lexica

Ibn Manzūr, Muḥammad b. Mukarram, *Lisān al-ʿarab* (Beirut: Dār al-Ṣādir, 1414/1994).

Lane, Edward W., *An Arabic-English Lexicon* (Beirut: Librairie du Liban, 1997 [Edinburgh: Williams and Norgate, 1863]).

al-Zabīdi, Murtaḍā Muḥammad b. Muḥammad, *Tāj al-ʿArūs* (Beirut: Dar al-Fikr, 1414/1994).

Arabic editions of Tabari's works

Tahdhīb al-āthār, vol. 4: *Musnad ʿAlī b. Abī Ṭālib* (ed. Maḥmūd Muḥammad Shākir; Cairo: Maṭbaʿat al-Madanī, 1982).

Ikhtilāf al-fuqahāʾ (ed. Friedrich Kern; Cairo, 1902).

Jāmiʿ al-bayān ʿan taʾwīl ay al-Qurʾān (ed. Ṣidqī Ḥamīd al-ʿAṭṭār; Beirut: Dār al-Fikr, 1995).

Taʾrīkh al-umam wa-l-muluk (Beirut: Dār al-Kutub al-ʿIlmiyya, 1997).

Translations of Tabari's works

Nöldeke, Theodor, *Geschichte der Perser und Araber zur Zeit der Sasaniden. Aus der arabischen Chronik des Ṭabarī. Übersetzt und mit ausführlichen Erläuterungen und Ergänzungen versehen von Th. Nöldeke* (Leiden: E. J. Brill, 1979 [Graz: Akademische Druck- und Verlagsanstalt, 1973]).

Godé, Pierre, *Abū Jaʿfar Muḥammad Ibn Jarīr aṭ-Ṭabarī: Commentaire du Coran. Abrégé, traduit et annoté par Pierre Godé* (Paris : Éditions d'art les heures claires, 1986).

Cooper, John, *The Commentary on the Qurʾān by Abū Jaʿfar Muḥammad b. Jarīr al-Ṭabarī. Being an abridged translation of Jāmiʿ al-bayān ʿan taʾwīl ay al-Qurʾān with an Introduction and Notes by J. Cooper* (General editors W. F. Madelung and A. Jones, vol. 1; Oxford: Oxford University Press, 1987).

Ibrahim, Yasir S., *al-Tabari's Book of Jihad: a Translation from the Original Arabic* (Lewiston, New York: Edwin Mellen Press, 2007).

Translations of the History

The translation of the *History* came about through the efforts of Ehsan Yar Shater. It comprises some 6300 pages, excluding translators' notes and commentary. Work on the translation began in 1974, using the Leiden edition of the Arabic text (1879–1901; 13 vols. plus index and supplement) by a team of scholars under the supervision of the Dutch Orientalist M. J. de Goeje. For the English translation the Leiden text was divided into appropriate portions and each assigned to an expert on the period in case. A total of thirty scholars served as translators under the general editorship of Ehsan Yar Shater. The resulting 40 volumes (listed in numerical order below) were published between 1985 and 2007 by the State University of New York Press. Of these 40 volumes, 1–38 deal with history proper. Vol. 39 is Tabari's supplement, listing the scholars who make up his source references; vol. 40 is an index to the whole *History*.

1. *General Introduction and From the Creation to the Flood* (Franz Rosenthal, 1989).
2. *Prophets and Patriarchs* (William M. Brinner, 1987).
3. *The Children of Israel* (William M. Brinner, 1991).
4. *The Ancient Kingdoms* (Moshe Perlmann, 1987).
5. *The Sasanids, the Byzantines, the Lakhmids, and Yemen* (C. E. Bosworth, 1999).

6. *Muḥammad at Mecca*
(W. Montgomery Watt and M. V. McDonald, 1988).
7. *The Foundation of the Community*
(M. V. McDonald and W. Montgomery Watt, 1987).
8. *The Victory of Islam* (Michael Fishbein, 1997).
9. *The Last Years of the Prophet* (Ismail K. Poonawala, 1990).
10. *The Conquest of Arabia* (Fred M. Donner, 1993).
11. *The Challenge to the Empires* (Khalid Y. Blankinship, 1993).
12. *The Battle of al-Qādisiyya and the Conquest of Syria and Palestine* (Yohanan Friedmann, 1992).
13. *The Conquest of Iraq, Southwestern Persia, and Egypt*
(Gautier H. A. Juynboll, 1989).
14. *The Conquest of Iran* (G. Rex Smith, 1994).
15. *The Crisis of the Early Caliphate*
(R. Stephen Humphreys, 1990).
16. *The Community Divided* (Adrian Brockett, 1997).
17. *The First Civil War* (G. R. Hawting, 1996).
18. *Between Civil Wars: The Caliphate of Muʿāwiya*
(Michael G. Morony, 1987).
19. *The Caliphate of Yazīd b. Muʿāwiya*
(I. K. A. Howard, 1990).
20. *The Collapse of Sufyanid Authority and the Coming of the Marwanids* (G. R. Hawting, 1989).
21. *The Victory of the Marwanids* (Michael Fishbein, 1990).
22. *The Marwanid Restoration* (Everett K. Rowson, 1989).
23. *The Zenith of the Marwanid House* (Martin Hinds, 1990).
24. *The Empire in Transition* (David Stephan Powers, 1989).
25. *The End of Expansion* (Khalid Yahya Blankinship, 1989).
26. *The Waning of the Umayyad Caliphate*
(Carole Hillenbrand, 1989).
27. *The ʿAbbasid Revolution* (John Alden Williams, 1985).
28. *ʿAbbasid Authority Affirmed* (Jane D. McAuliffe, 1995).
29. *Al-Manṣūr and al-Mahdī* (Hugh Kennedy, 1990).
30. *The ʿAbbasid Caliphate in Equilibrium*
(C. E. Bosworth, 1989).
31. *The War between Brothers* (Michael Fishbein, 1992).

32. *The Reunification of the Abbasid Caliphate* (C. E. Bosworth, 1987).
33. *Storm and Stress along the Northern Frontiers of the ʿAbbasid Caliphate* (C. E. Bosworth, 1991).
34. *Incipient Decline* (Joel L. Kraemer, 1989).
35. *The Crisis of the ʿAbbasid Caliphate* (George Saliba, 1985).
36. *The Revolt of the Zanj* (David Waines, 1992).
37. *The ʿAbbasid Recovery* (Philip M. Fields, 1987).
38. *The Return of the Caliphate to Baghdad* (Franz Rosenthal, 1985).
39. *Biographies of the Prophet's Companions and Their Successors* (Ella Landau-Tasseron, 1998).
40. *Index* (Alex V. Popovkin and Everett K. Rowson, 2007).

General works

Abbott, Nabia, *Studies in Arabic Literary Papyrii, I: Historical Texts*, Oriental Institute Publications 75 (Chicago: University of Chicago Press, 1957).

Afsaruddin, Asma, *Excellence & Precedence: Medieval Islamic Discourse on Legitimate Leadership* (Leiden: Brill, 2002).

Al-Azmeh, Aziz, *The Times of History: Universal Topics in Islamic Historiography* (Budapest: Central European University Press, 2007).

Ben Shemesh, A., *Taxation in Islam. Vol. III: Abu Yusuf's Kitab al-Kharaj, Translated and Provided with an Introduction and Notes* (Leiden: Brill, 1969).

Bosworth, C. E., 'The Armies of the Saffarids', *Bulletin of the School of Oriental and African Studies*, 31/3 (1968): 534–54.

——, 'al-Ṭabarī' (1998), *Encyclopaedia of Islam* (2nd edn.), ii. 11–15.

——, 'The Persian Contribution to Islamic Historiography in the Pre-Mongol Period' in R. G. Hovannisian and G. Sabagh (eds.), *The Persian Presence in the Islamic World* (Cambridge: Cambridge University Press, 1998): 218–36.

Bowen, Harold, *The Life and Times of ʿAlī ibn ʿIsā 'The Good Vizier'* (Cambridge: Cambridge University Press, 1928).

Busse, Heribert, '"Omar b. al-Khaṭṭāb in Jerusalem', *Jerusalem Studies in Arabic and Islam*, 5 (1984): 73–119.

——, '"Umar's Image as the Conqueror of Jerusalem', *Jerusalem Studies in Arabic and Islam*, 8 (1986): 149–68.

Calder, Norman, '*Tafsir* from Tabari to Ibn Kathir: Problems in the Description of a Genre, Illustrated with Reference to the Story of Abraham' in Hawting and Shareef (1993): 101–40.

de Certeau, Michel, *L'Écriture de l'histoire* (Paris: Éditions Gallimard, 1975). English transl.: Tom Conley, *The Writing of History* (New York: Columbia University Press, 1988).

Cook, Michael, *The Koran: A Very Short Introduction* (Oxford: Oxford University Press, 2000).

Daftary, Farhad, *The Isma'ilis: Their History and Doctrines* (Cambridge: Cambridge University Press, 1990).

——, *Ismailis in Medieval Muslim Societies* (London: I. B. Tauris, 2005).

Daniel, Elton, 'The Samanid "Translations" of al-Tabari' in Hugh Kennedy (2008): 263–97.

Duri, 'Abd al-'Aziz, *The Rise of Historical Writing Among the Arabs*. (Ed. and transl., Lawrence I. Conrad; Princeton, NJ: Princeton University Press, 1983).

Elazar, Daniel J., *The Covenant Tradition in Politics: 1. Covenant & Polity in Israel; 2. Covenant & Commonwealth; 3. Covenant and Constitutionalism* (New Brunswick: Transaction Publishers Inc., 1995–98).

El-Hibri, Tayeb (1999a), *Reinterpreting Islamic Historiography: Hārūn al-Rashīd and the Narrative of the ʿAbbasid Caliphate* (Cambridge: Cambridge University Press, 1999).

—— (1999b), 'The Unity of Tabari's Chronicle', *al-ʿUṣūr al-wusṭā. The Bulletin of Middle East Medievalists*, 11/1 (1999): 1–3.

Daniel, Elton, 'The Samanid "Translations" of al-Tabari' in Hugh Kennedy (2008): 263–97.

Forand, Guy, 'The Status of the Land and Inhabitants of the Sawad during the First Two Centuries of Islam', *Journal of the Economic and Social History of the Orient*, 14 (1971): 25–37.

Frye, Richard N., *The History of Ancient Iran* (Munich: C. H. Beck, 1984).

Gilliot, Claude, 'Portrait 'mythique' d'Ibn ʿAbbās', *Arabica: Révue des Études Arabes*, 32 (1985) : 127–84.

——, *Exégèse, langue et théologie en Islam. L' Exégèse coranique de Tabari (m. 311/923)*, Études Musulmanes 32 (Paris: Librairie Philosophique J. Vrin, 1990).

——, 'Mythe, recit, histoire du salut dans le commentaire coranique de Ṭabarī', *Journal Asiatique*, 282/2 (1994) : 237–70.

Gordon, Matthew S., 'The Khaqanid Families of the Early ʿAbbasid Period', *Journal of the American Oriental Society*, 121/2 (April–June, 2001): 236–55.

Guillaume, Alfred, *The Life of Muḥammad: a Translation of Ibn Isḥāq's* Sīrat Rasūl Allāh (Karachi: Oxford University Press, 1995 [1955]).

Haji, Hamid, *Founding the Fatimid State: The Rise of an Early Islamic Empire: An Annotated English Translation of al-Qāḍī al-Nuʿmān's* Iftitāḥ al-daʿwa (London: I. B. Tauris, 2006).

Hawting, G. R. and Abdul-Kader Shareef (eds.), *Approaches to the Qur'an* (London/New York: Routledge, 1993).

Heck, Gene W., 'Gold Mining in Arabia and the Rise of the Islamic State', *Journal of the Economic and Social History of the Orient*, 42/3 (1999): 364–95.

Hinds, Martin, 'The Siffin Arbitration Agreement', *Journal of Semitic Studies*, 17 (1972): 93–113.

Hodgson, Marshal G. S., *The Venture of Islam. Conscience and History in a World Civilization*, vol. 1 (Chicago: University of Chicago Press, 1974).

——, 'Two Pre-Modern Historians: Pitfalls and Opportunities in Presenting Them to Moderns' in J. U. Nef (ed.), *Towards World Community*, World Academy of Arts and Sciences Publications, 5 (The Hague: Dr. W. Junk N. V. Publishers, 1968): 53–68.

Humphreys, R. Stephen, 'Qur'anic Myth and Narrative Structure in Early Islamic Historiography' in F. M. Clover and R. S. Humphreys (eds.), *Tradition and Innovation in Late*

Antiquity (Madison: University of Wisconsin Press, 1989): 271–90.

Hylén, Torsten, *Ḥusayn, the Mediator: A Structural Analysis of the Karbalaʾ Drama according to Abū Jaʿfar Muḥammad b. Jarīr al-Ṭabarī (d. 310/923)*, unpublished dissertation (Uppsala University, 2007).

Ibn Ḥazm, ʿAlī b. Aḥmad b. Saʿīd, *al-Fisal fi l-milal wa-l-ahwa wa-l-nihal*, vols. 1–5 (Beirut: Dār al-Maʿrifa, 1975).

Kennedy, Hugh (ed.), *Al-Tabarī: A Medieval Muslim Historian and His Work*. Studies in Late Antiquity and Early Islam, 15 (Princeton, NJ: The Darwin Press, Inc., 2008).

——, *The Prophet and the Age of the Caliphates: The Islamic Near East from the Sixth to the Eleventh Century* (London/New York: Longman, 1986).

——, 'The Financing of the Military in the Early Islamic State' in Averil Cameron (ed.), *The Byzantine and Early Islamic Near East. III: States, Resources and Armies*, (Princeton, NJ: The Darwin Press, 1995): 361–78.

——, *The Early Abbasid Caliphate: A Political History* (London: Croom Helm, 1981).

——, 'Central Government and Provincial Élites and the Early ʿAbbasid Caliphate', *Bulletin of the School of Oriental and African Studies* 44 (1981): 26–38.

——, 'Caliphs and their Chroniclers in the Middle Abbasid period (third/ninth century)', in D. S. Richards and Chase F. Robinson (eds.), *Texts, Documents and Artefacts: Islamic Studies in Honour of D. S. Richards* (Leiden: Brill, 2003): 17–35.

Khalidi, Tarif, *Arabic Historical Thought in the Classical Period* (Cambridge: Cambridge University Press, 1994).

Landau-Tasseron, Ella, 'Sayf ibn ʿUmar in Medieval and Modern Scholarship', *Der Islam* 67 (1990): 1–26.

——, 'From Tribal Society to Centralized Polity: An Interpretation of Events and Anecdotes of the Formative Period of Islam', *Jerusalem Studies of Arabic and Islam* 24 (2000): 180–216.

Lewy, Hildegard, 'The Genesis of the Faulty Persian Chronology', *Journal of the American Oriental Society*, 64/4 (1944): 197–214.

Løkkegaard, Frede, *Islamic Taxation in the Classic Period with Special Reference to Circumstances in Iraq* (Copenhagen: Branner og Korch, 1950).

Madelung, Wilferd, 'Imāma' (1971), *Encyclopaedia of Islam* (2nd edn.), iii. 1163–9.

—— and Paul E. Walker (eds. and transl.), *The Advent of the Fatimids: A Contemporary Shiʿi Witness* (London: I. B. Tauris, 2001).

McAuliffe, Jane D., 'Al-Tabari's Prelude to the Prophet' in Hugh Kennedy (2008): 113–29.

——, 'Quranic Hermeneutics: The Views of al-Ṭabarī and Ibn Kathīr', in Andrew Rippin (ed.), *Approaches to the Interpretation of the Qur'an* (Oxford: Clarendon Press, 1988): 46–62.

——, 'al-Tabari's Prelude to the Prophet' in Hugh Kennedy (2008): 113–29.

Melchert, Christopher, *The Formation of the Sunni Schools of Law, 9th –10th Centuries CE.* (Leiden: Brill, 1997).

Morony, Michael G., *Iraq after the Muslim Conquest* (Princeton, NJ: Princeton University Press, 1984).

Muth, F-C., *Die Annalen von aṭ-Ṭabarī im Spiegel der europäischen Bearbeitungen*, Heidelberger orientalistische Studien, 5 (Frankfurt am Main: Peter Lang, 1983).

Mårtensson, Ulrika, 'The True New Testament: Sealing the Heart's Covenant in al-Ṭabarī's *Taʾrīkh al-rusul wa-l-muluk*', PhD dissertation, Uppsala University (2001).

——, 'Discourse and Historical Analysis: The Case of al-Ṭabarī's History of the Messengers and the Kings,' *Journal of Islamic Studies*, 16/3 (2005): 287–331.

——, 'The Persuasive Proof:' A Study of Aristotle's Politics and Rhetoric in the Qur'an and al-Tabari's Commentary', *Jerusalem Studies in Arabic and Islam*, 34 (2008) [56 pp.].

Nagel, Tilman, *The History of Islamic Theology: From Muḥammad to the Present* (Princeton, NJ: Markus Wiener Publishers, 2000).

Newby, Gordon D., *The Making of the Last Prophet: A Reconstruction of the Earliest Biography of Muḥammad* (South Carolina: University of South Carolina Press, 1989).

Petersen, Erling L., *ʿAlī and Muʿāwiya in Early Arabic Tradition: Studies on the Genesis and Growth of Islamic Historical Writing until the End of the Ninth Century* (Copenhagen: Munksgaard, 1964).

Popovic, Alexandre, *La Révolte des esclaves en Iraq au IIIe/IXe Siècle* (Paris: Geuthner, 1976).

Radtke, Bernd, 'Towards a Typology of Abbasid Universal Chronicles', in D. E. P. Jackson *et al.* (eds.), *Occasional Papers of the School of Abbasid Studies*, 3 (1990): 1–18.

Roberts, Joseph B., 'Early Islamic Historiography: Ideology and Methodology' (PhD thesis, The Ohio State University, 1986).

Robinson, Chase F., *Islamic Historiography* (Cambridge: Cambridge University Press, 2004).

Rosenthal, Franz, 'The Influence of the Biblical Tradition on Muslim Historiography,' in B. Lewis and P. M. Holt (eds.), *Historical Writings of the Peoples of Asia 4: Historians of the Middle East* (London: Oxford University Press, 1962): 35–45.

——, *A History of Muslim Historiography* (2nd edn., Leiden: Brill, 1968).

Rubin, Uri, 'Exegesis and *Hadith*: The Case of the Seven *Mathanī*' in Hawting and Shareef (1993): 141–56.

Rubin, Zeev, 'Al-Tabari and the Age of the Sasanians' in Hugh Kennedy (2008): 41–71.

——, 'The Reforms of Khusro Anushirwan' in A. Cameron (ed.), *The Byzantine and Early Islamic Near East. III: States, Resources and Armies*, (Princeton, New Jersey: The Darwin Press, Inc., 1995): 227–97.

Shoshan, Boaz, *Poetics of Islamic Historiography: Deconstructing Ṭabarī's History* (Leiden: Brill, 2004).

von Sivers, Peter, 'Taxes and Trade in the 'Abbasid Thughūr, 750–962/133–351', *Journal of the Economic and Social History of the Orient*, 25/1 (1982): 71–99.

Sourdel, Dominique, *Le Vizirat ʿAbbaside de 749 à 936 (132 à 324 de l'Hégire)*. (Damascus: Institut Français de Damas, vol. 1, 1959 ; vol. 2, 1960).

——, 'Une Profession de Foi de l'Historien al-Ṭabarī', *Revue des études islamiques* 26 (1968): 177–99.

Tayob, Abdelkader I., 'An Analytical Survey of al-Ṭabarī's Exegesis of the Cultural Symbolic Construct of *fitna*' in Hawting and Shareef (1993): 157–72.

——, 'Ṭabarī on the Companions of the Prophet: Moral and Political Contours in Islamic Historical Writing', *Journal of the American Oriental Society*, 119/2 (April–June, 1999): 203–10.

Tottolli, Roberto, *Biblical Prophets in the Qurʾān and Muslim Literature* (Richmond: Curzon Press, 2002).

Turner, John P., 'The *abnāʾ al-dawla*: The Definition and Legitimation of Identity in Response to the Fourth *fitna*', *Journal of the American Oriental Society*, 124/1 (January–March, 2004): 1–22.

Vali, Abbas, *Pre-capitalist Iran: A Theoretical History* (London: I. B. Tauris, 1993).

Vasmer, A. [– C. E. Bosworth], 'Māzandarān' (1990), *Encyclopaedia of Islam* (2nd edn.), vi. 935–42.

Wasserstrom, Steven M., *Between Muslim and Jew: The Problem of Symbiosis under Early Islam* (Princeton, NJ: Princeton University Press, 1995).

Wellhausen, Julius, *The Arab Kingdom and its Fall* (London: Curzon Press Ltd., 1973).

Zakeri, Mohsen, 'Al-Tabari on Sasanian History: A Study in Sources' in Hugh Kennedy (2008): 27–40.

Index

'Abbasid: caliphate, 1, 6; empire, 3, 6, 9–13, 27, 30–1, 36–7, 40, 43–7, 53, 56–9, 92, 124–9, 134–8, 141, 143, 145–8, 155, 157, 161–8; *see also: Maps*, 10, 14, 123

'Abbasid caliphs: Abu l-'Abbas 'al-Saffah', 137; al-Amin, 138, 158; Harun al-Rashid, 158, 163; al-Ma'mun, 137–41, 158; al-Mahdi, 44, 47, 59, 92, 138; al-Mutawakkil, 140, 158; al-Mansur, 59; al-Mu'tadid, 44, 143; al-Mu'tamid, 44; al-Muktafi, 45; al-Muqtadir, 45

'Abd al-Rahman b. 'Awf, 72, 102

abnāʾ al-dawla, 138, 168

abnāʾ Khūrasān, 11

Abraham, 50, 56–7, 60–1, 82, 95, 110, 163; Sarah, Hagar, 81

Abū Jaʿfar (al-Tabari), 3, 7–8, 16, 160, 165

Abu Talib, Prophet's uncle, 97

Adam, 51, 56, 61, 75–7, 81, 95, 154

ʿahd, 39, 48–50, 53, 78–9, 114, 120, 131, 135–6, 148

'Alid(s): 3, 8–9, 12–13, 15, 123, 125–6, 129–30, 134–8, 140–8; Hasan b. 'Ali, 121–3, 130, 134; Hasanid 'Alids, 9; Hasan b. 'Ali al-Utrush, 144; Muhammad b. Ward, 143; Husayn b. 'Ali, 124, 130–6, 156–8, 163; Husaynid 'Alids, 9; Zayd b. 'Ali, 8, 13, 134; Zaydi(s), 9, 109; Yahya b. 'Umar, 141

'Amr b. al-'As, 110, 113, 119, 121

Alexander 'the Great', 6, 83

Amul, 8, 11

Arabian Peninsula, 42, 56, 94, 100, 102
Arabic: 6, 9, 15–17, 20, 23–4, 26, 35, 51, 59, 73, 80, 84, 90, 96, 124, 127–8, 150, 154, 156, 159–60, 165, 167; Qur'anic: 24–5, 32, 48
Aristotle, 52–3, 148, 168
al-Ash'ari, theologian, 17, 147–8
attributes (of God), 18, 22–3
Avesta, 37, 83;

Babylon, 77, 147, 94
Baghdad, 11–13, 46–7, 56, 59, 122, 129, 138, 141, 143, 159, 162
Banu Tahir, vassals, 141–3
Basra, 11, 108, 115, 117, 126, 130
Battles: Badr, 29; the Camel ('A'isha, Talha, al-Zubayr), 115–16; Dhu Qar, 91; Karbala, 131–4, 165; Qadisiyya, 103–4, 107, 161; Siffin, 117, 158, 164; *see Map*, 101
Bible, the 48–9, 53, 57–65
Byzantine(s), 46, 56, 62, 92–4, 97, 103, 106, 122, 138–9, 157, 160, 165, 167; *see also: Map*, 99

calendar: Greek, 83; imperial time, 105; Islamic, 36, 56, 76, 100, 104; Persian, 83–4
caliphate, 1, 9, 12–13, 21, 31, 33, 36–8, 40, 42–4, 46–7, 53, 56, 58–9, 102–4, 109–10, 112–13, 117–18, 120–5, 127, 129–30, 134, 136–8, 140, 147, 154, 161–3, 165
Christ, 48, 128; Christianity, 2, 30, 60, 94, 96, 126, 128, 139, 155; Christians, 28–9, 41–2, 48
civil war (*fitna*), 56, 111, 116–17, 152, 168
Commander of the Faithful, 21, 44, 78, 140
Companion(s): 6, 18, 20–1, 28–9, 33, 104, 111, 156, 161, 165; traditions, 1, 20, 21, 27, 33, 34
Companion caliphs: Abu Bakr, 21, 33–4, 56–7, 100, 102–3, 109–11, 115, 118, 126, 130, 158; 'Umar b. al-Khattab, 21, 63, 102–4, 106–7, 111–12, 116, 118, 139–40, 142, 163; 'Uthman b. 'Affan, 21, 32–4, 42, 49, 56–7, 103, 108–22, 125, 132, 146, 154, 156; 'Ali b. Abi Talib, 8, 12, 21, 34, 38, 42, 47, 49, 56–7, 62–3, 74, 92, 104, 108–32, 134, 137, 140, 143, 156
Constantinople, 2, 106

contract, 4, 39, 48–3, 67, 74, 78–9, 83–4, 96, 114, 119–20, 130–1, 135–6, 148–9; social contract: 91–3, 146
covenant, 4, 39, 48–53, 58, 60, 63–4, 66–7, 70, 78–82, 84–5, 89, 93, 95, 108, 110, 114, 120, 134–6, 149, 154, 164, 166; constitution, 52–3, 55, 100, 149, 163

Daylam, 142
deeds, 21, 22, 117, 121
Dhayl al-mudhayyal, 69
Dome of the Rock, the 123, 125
dynastic: rule, 21, 102; succession, 21, 122–6

Egypt, 11, 81, 110, 113, 115, 121, 125, 161
election, 21
Emigrants, 29, 49, 114
epistemology, 16, 18, 25, 128, 147; idealism, 16, 17, 32, 128; empiricism, 16–19, 25, 32–4, 54, 70
faith, 1, 21, 117, 121, 128, 152
Fars, 46, 77, 81, 84, 146
Fatima, 12, 31, 118, 126, 131, 133
Fatimid(s), 13, 30, 31, 46, 126, 164, 166

Gabriel, 95, 98
God's Messenger, 19, 29, 34, 51, 102
Gospel, the, 96
Greek philosophy, 16
ḥadīth, 1, 34

Hashim(i), 62, 94, 108, 122, 133, 136–8
Helpers, the, 29, 49, 114
Hijaz, 42, 91, 93, 121, 125
Hijra, 62, 75–6, 93, 100
History, 36–9 *et passim*: socio-political and legal context, 40–54; chronology, 55–6; biblical contents, 57–65; myth and time, 70–81; the covenant (Abraham, Moses, the Persian kings), 81–93; the Prophet, 93–100; the Companion caliphs, 101–22; the dynastic caliphates, 122–5; the 'Alids and the state, 125–45
History, passages cited from, 47, 49, 51, 57, 59, 60–1, 66, 71, 75–80, 83, 88, 94–5, 103–6, 108–9, 115, 127–9, 131–7, 139–41, 144
historians: Abu Mikhnaf, 117, 119–20, 130, 132–5, 155–7; Ibn Hisham, 59; Ibn Humayd, 60; Ibn Ishaq (biographer of the

Prophet), 59–60, 82, 90, 97–8, 114, 139; Muhammad b. Sahl, 126; Salama b. al-Fadl, 60; Sayf b. 'Umar, 113–15, 125, 155–6, 165; Wahb b. Munabbih, 58, 59; al-Waqidi, 102, 110–11, 113–14, 156; Yunus b. Bukayr, 60
Hour (the Last), 26, 72, 75–6
Hudaybiyya, treaty of, 29

Iblīs, 79–80
Ibn 'Abbas, 'Abdallah, 27–8, 32, 51, 60, 72, 76, 83, 109–10, 117, 130, 139
Ibn al-Muqaffa', 87
Ibn al-Zubayr, 78, 130, 132–3
Ibn Hanbal, Ahmad, 15, 18–20, 22, 33–5
Ibn Hazm (theologian), 17–18
Ibn Jarir (al-Tabari), 7, 9, 160
Ibn Ziyad, 'Ubayd Allah, 130, 132
idolatry (*shirk*), 17, 29, 100
Imam: 13, 21, 31–2, 111; 'Alid: 125, 134, 138; the hidden, 31, 128
Imami Shi'i(s), 15, 118, 146
infidel, unbeliever (*kāfir*), 18, 129; unbelief (*kufr*), 33
innovation (*bidʿa*), 17, 22, 29–30
inquisition (*miḥna*), 138, 140
Iraq, 13, 29, 59, 104, 110, 113, 121, 125, 134, 161, 166–7
Isaac (Isḥāq), 57, 61, 81
Ishmael, 81, 95, 105
Isma'il(is): 28, 30–2, 43, 93, 129, 163; *daʿwa* 13; 'Abbasid campaigns against, 46; interpretation, propaganda, 31; line of, 13; rebellions led by, 43; and Saba'i(s), 28; Shi'i leadership, 129
Israelite(s): 36, 55, 57, 60, 76, 106, 154; covenant, 49; kingdom(s), 36–7; kingship, 57, 106; messengers and kings, 36; people, 83–4, 96; people and covenant, 149; prophethood, 56, 154; prophets, 60, 76
Israelite kings, 55; David, 37, 50, 57, 63–5, 100, 106; Solomon, 57, 106
Ja'far al-Sadiq (Ja'fari), 13, 15, 18, 146, 151
Jayumart, 76–7, 80, 146
Jerusalem, 61, 94, 106, 124, 163
Jesus, 26, 28, 31, 57, 60, 64–5, 98, 128, 139; *see also:* Christ

Jews (Judaism), 28–30, 41–2, 48, 60, 62, 64, 75, 94–5, 106
jihad, 32, 35, 117, 126, 151, 160
Judgement Day, 28, 36
judges, 8, 88, 138–9
jurisprudence, 1, 3, 12, 15, 18–19, 152
jurists: Abu Hanifa, 36; Abu Yusuf, 42, 161; al-Awza'i, 36; Malik b. Anas, 36; al-Shafi'i, 36
justice, 2, 31, 52, 58, 65, 80–1, 86, 89, 97, 107, 118, 127, 129, 144

Ka'b al-Ahbar, 58, 82, 106
Ka'ba, 60–1, 77–8, 81, 94–6, 107, 124, 134
Khadija, Prophet's wife, 56, 95, 96
khalīfa (pl. *khulafā'*), 59, 102
Khariji(s), 21, 28–30, 119–21, 125–7, 137
Khurasan, 11, 43, 137–8, 141–2
king lists, 36, 76, 83–4
kingship, 21, 55–8, 63, 70, 76, 82, 104, 106, 122, 146–7, 154
kitāb (written document), 27, 49, 52, 119, 135, 149
Kufa, 11, 13, 59, 80, 115, 117, 121, 123, 127, 130–7, 142–3

Lakhmid kings, 91, 94, 126, 160; Hîra', 62; al-Nu'man b. al-Mundhir, 91
land, 4, 40–2, 44, 48, 83, 85–9, 91–2, 104–5, 110; of Canaan, 60, 64; in Madina, 135; ownership *vs.* use of, 40, 142–3; the promised, 48, 58, 63, 83, 103; survey, 87; tax on, 40–2, 44, 85–9, 91–2, 110, 158, 161; *see also:* tax
language: analysis, 26; God's, 24; God's, esoteric, 32; Qur'anic, 24, 153; theory of, 23–4, 32, 54, 145, 148, 153
al-Laṭīf fi aḥkām sharā'iʿ al-Islām, 36
law(s), 4, 8, 18, 38–9, 44, 48–53, 62, 65, 80–4, 94, 96, 100, 105, 108, 111, 114, 145, 149, 151–2; schools of: Hanafi, 18, 42; Hanbali 12, 15, 17–23, 35, 47, 117, 138, 146–49, 152; Jariri , 36, 151; Maliki, 18
lawgiver, 52, 61
logos, Logos,128

Madina, 24, 28–9, 56, 58–9, 64, 75, 90, 93, 95, 101–2, 109, 113, 115, 122, 124, 130, 134–6, 143
Makka, 24, 51, 56, 60–1, 63, 75, 77–8, 81, 93, 95–6,

100, 115, 129, 130, 132, 143, 161
Mary, 26, 31, 49, 64, 128
Mazandaran, 8, 168
merit: 20–1; basis of, 21, 102, 105, 122–3, 126, 146; by belonging in Islam, 105
Mesopotamia, 2, 40, 57, 60, 79, 94, 122, 127, 146
Messengers, 24–5, 28, 36, 53, 55, 57, 60, 70, 76, 96
Messiah, son of Mary, 49, 106
messianic: kingship, 106; symbolism, 103
methodology, 2–5, 16–17, 19, 32, 38, 54–5, 65, 70, 152–3, 167
mīthāq, 39, 48–51, 53, 79, 114, 136, 149; *mīthāq al-kitāb*, 49
Moses, 48–50, 57–8, 61–5, 82, 83–4, 95–6
Most Beautiful Names, 18, 23
muḥkamāt, 27–8
muṣḥaf, 34
Muhammad, the Prophet, 28, 51, 57, 83, 95, 96, 109
muqāsama, 44, 46, 87, 92
Musnad (Ibn Hanbal), 33–4
mutashābihāt, 27–8

Nestorian, 41, 45, 59, 94, 155
Noah, 48, 50, 57, 60, 61, 81

Pen, the, 71–2, 75
Persian kings, 37, 55, 76, 81, 83–4, 87, 92, 149, 157; Biwarasb, 80–1; al-Dahhak, 80–1, 119; Kay Qubadh, 87; Manushihr, 84–6, 89, 92; Oshahanj, 79–81
philosophy, 15–16, 129, 148
pilgrimage (*hajj*): 51, 55, 67, 78, 81–2, 95, 108, 110, 129, 134; stations of, 78
Plato, 52, 122, 148
predestination, 5, 20, 72-3; free will, 5, 20, 74
Prophet, the, 11–12, 17–18, 21, 24, 26–30, 33–4, 45, 47, 49, 52, 55–65, 74–6, 81–3, 90, 93–100, 102, 103, 108–15, 118, 122, 124–6, 132–7, 142, 145–6, 150, 155–7, 161, 165–8; biography of, 15; traditions of, 1, 3, 11, 17–18, 20–1, 23, 26, 30, 33, 35–6, 39, 72, 74
prophets, 36, 48, 55, 57, 60, 68, 79, 98, 157, 160, 168

qadar, 72–3, 75
Qarmat(ians), 13, 15, 30, 43, 46, 127–9
Qur'an(ic), 1, 3, 9, 15, 17–18, 20, 22–3, 26–8, 30, 32–3, 36, 39, 47–9, 51–3, 61, 96, 116, 119, 128, 138–40, 147–9;

interpretation, 1, 3, 9, 15, 23, 26–7, 149, 152–4, 156, 164, 166; Isma'ili interpretation, 31; theory, practice of, 23–4, 26

reason(ing): 16–19, 32, 66–7, 70, 75, 92; analogical, 18, 53; deductive, 69, 70; historical, 69; *istidlāl*, 17; *naẓar*, 20
reports (*khabar*, *akhbār*), 2–3, 8, 34, 36, 38, 58–61, 69, 72, 75, 81, 83–5, 93, 95, 98, 103, 106, 109, 113–15, 126–9, 134–5, 143–6, 154–8
Resurrection, Day of, 51, 72, 112

Sa'd b. Abi Waqqas, 103, 108
sabʿat aḥruf, 33
Saba'i(s), 28–30, 113, 115, 125
Saffarid(s), 46, 162
Samanid(s), 46, 147, 157, 163
Sassanid(s), 1–2, 8–10, 37, 40–2, 55–6, 83–4, 87, 89–91, 94, 97, 103–4, 107–9, 126, 147, 151, 153; Ardashir I, 83; Hurmuz, 89, 90; Khusraw Anushirwan, 87–93, 104, 142; Khusraw Parviz, 90–93, 109; Yazdagird III, 84
Satanic verses, 97
Sawad, the, 6, 41, 42, 45, 58, 80, 81, 84, 103, 127, 129, 142, 165
scribes, 44, 50, 155; Banu al-Furat, 45; Banu al-Jarrah, 11, 45, 47; the Khaqan(s), 11–12; Zayd b. Thabit, the Prophet's scribe, 33
Shafi'i, law, 15, 18, 148, 151
Shi'i(s), Shi'a, 12, 28, 31, 102, 109, 125–6, 129, 133–4, 141, 144, 146, 153, 157
Siyar muluk al-ʿajam, 84, 87
state administration, 3, 11, 42, 44, 47, 51, 88, 92, 105, 124–5, 134, 144–6, 158
succession, 2, 4, 21, 37–8, 57, 68, 122, 125
Syria, 2, 29, 57, 94, 106, 111, 115, 122, 161

Tabari: *passim*; his life, 7–15; methodology, 15–19, 65–70, 152–8; works: *Jami'*, 1, 23–34, 49, 53, 60, 94, 145, 147–8, 152, 157; *Ikhtilaf*, 1, 35–6, 53, 159; *Sarih al-sunna*, 19–23, 122, 151; *Tahdhib*, 1, 34–5, 53, 74, 159; *Ta'rikh*: *see History*
Tabaristan, 8–9, 11, 13, 37, 76, 109, 142–4, 147; Mt. Dunbawand, 77, 147

tax: 4, 80–1, 91–2, 104, 125, 146; collectors, 71, 88; revenue, 41–2, 44–6, 86–8, 110, 121, 139, 145–67, 158, 162, 166, 168
theology (*kalām*), 4, 12, 15, 17, 20, 32, 73, 129, 148, 151–3; schools of: Ash'ari, 17, 147–8; Jabriyya, 73; Jahmiyya, 22; Mu'tazila, 17–22, 138, 147; Murji'a, 19, 20, 21; Qadariyya, 19, 30, 73
Throne (of God), 22–3, 72, 77–8
tradition, 4, 16, 18, 21, 23, 26, 34–6, 69, 74, 152; *āthār*, 20
tribes, 6, 13, 33, 43, 50, 93, 102, 105; 'Abd al-Qays, 126–7; 'Aws, 63, 100; Banu Hashim, 108; Khazraj, 63, 100; Quraysh, 56, 61–4, 94–6, 97, 98–100, 102, 122, 140

Umayyad(s), 3, 6, 56–8, 108, 125, 134–8, 157, 161; Banu Marwan, Banu Sufyan: 122–3
Umayyad caliphs: 'Abd al-Malik, 123, 125; Mu'awiya, 38, 78, 110–11, 115, 117, 119–23, 125, 129–31, 156, 160; Yazid b. Mu'awiya, 122, 129–31, 134, 157

vassal(age), 40–4, 48, 51, 58, 70, 84, 86–7, 91–4, 126, 141–2
vizier(s), 11, 44, 49, 92, 125, 140, 147; 'Ali b. 'Isa, 12, 45–7, 92; Hamid b. al-'Abbas, 45; Ibn al-Furat, 45–6; Ibn al-Khaqan, 46

Waraqa b. Nawfal, 64, 94, 96

Yemen, 2, 13, 57, 113, 115, 125, 160

Zanj, 13, 15, 43, 126–7, 129, 146, 162
Zoroaster, Zoroastrian(ism), 30, 37, 41, 83–5, 87, 94